Your Career and Life Plan *Portfolio*

Second Edition

- Explore and document your skills and values
- Review and organize your experiences and abilities
- Set a clear career direction and assess your progress
- Plan an effective job search campaign and present your portfolio in interviews
- Develop an action plan to get you where you want to go

By the Editors at JIST

Based on adult career development guidelines developed by the National Occupational Information Coordinating Committee

JIST *Works*

Your Career and Life Plan Portfolio, *Second Edition*

Previous edition was titled *Creating Your Life's Work Portfolio.*
© 2003 by JIST Publishing, Inc.

Published by JIST Works, an imprint of JIST Publishing, Inc.
8902 Otis Avenue
Indianapolis, IN 46216-1033
Phone: 800-648-JIST   Fax: 800-JIST-FAX
E-mail: info@jist.com   Web site: www.jist.com

Note to instructors. Support materials are available for *Your Career and Life Plan Portfolio.* An instructor's guide contains helpful guidance and many activities and assignments. Videos on portfolio development, resumes, and job search topics are also available. Call 1-800-648-JIST for details.

About career materials published by JIST. Our materials encourage people to be self-directed and to take control of their destinies. We work hard to provide excellent content, solid advice, and techniques that get results. If you have questions about this book or other JIST products, call 1-800-648-JIST or visit www.jist.com. For free occupational information, visit www.careeroink.com.

Quantity discounts are available for JIST products. Please call 1-800-648-JIST or visit www.jist.com for a free catalog and more information.

Visit www.jist.com. Find out about our products, get free book excerpts, order a catalog, and link to other career-related sites. You can also learn more about JIST authors and JIST training available to professionals.

Acquisitions Editor: Susan Pines
Contributing Writer: Judit E. Price
Development Editor: Veda Dickerson
Cover and Interior Designer: Aleata Howard
Page Layout Coordinator: Carolyn J. Newland
Proofreaders: David Faust, Jeanne Clark
Indexer: Jeanne Clark

Acknowledgment: The first and second JIST Publishing editions of this book are a complete revision of an earlier work titled *Life Work Portfolio.* The work was a joint project of the National Occupational Information Coordinating Committee (NOICC), the Maine Occupational Information Coordinating Committee, and the Career Development Training Institute at Oakland University. It was developed with an advisory committee representing job training, adult education, and displaced homemaker programs and was reviewed by a national review team comprising leaders in the career development field. The book was also pilot-tested at major universities, corporate sites, veterans affairs offices, job training programs, and community colleges. While the JIST Publishing editions incorporate major changes, they would not have been possible without the effort of the many people involved in the original *Life Work Portfolio* project.

Printed in the United States of America

08 07 06 05   9 8 7 6 5 4 3

We have been careful to provide accurate information throughout this book, but it is possible that errors and omissions have been introduced. Please consider this in making any career plans or other important decisions. Trust your own judgment above all else and in all things.

ISBN 1-56370-907-4

About This Book

Your portfolio is a collection of records that document your work history and affirm your successes. *Your Career and Life Plan Portfolio,* Second Edition, provides specific, basic information for gathering and displaying these records. But it does more than show you how to store documents. It explains a step-by-step process for making career decisions and developing career directions. It provides a structure for career planning that you can use more than once as your situation changes and as you grow and develop.

Your Career and Life Plan Portfolio can enable you to create a portfolio system that works for you. It describes the importance of keeping your portfolio up to date and helps you plan and make decisions as you face new challenges.

This book also gives you tips for being successful on your new job. It helps you understand what is important to you in your life and work, and it describes how information about yourself affects your job satisfaction.

TM

Table of Contents

Introduction to This Book

The purpose of a portfolio is to organize data you will need in your job search. The purpose of *Your Career and Life Plan Portfolio* is to provide you with the information you need for creating a portfolio, for making career decisions, and for approaching your life and your job search with confidence.

Overview

Your Career and Life Plan Portfolio is organized into three parts. Each part is divided into chapters. Here is an overview of each part.

Part One will benefit you in creating a portfolio for the first time or in updating and improving your existing portfolio. You'll find that Part One

- Defines what a portfolio is and explains why you need one

- Outlines the various types of portfolios

- Provides specific information on creating, organizing, and displaying your portfolio

- Describes the sections of a portfolio and what you might include in each section

- Explains how to use your portfolio in job interviews

- Includes directions for creating an electronic portfolio

Part Two will help you understand who you are and what you have to offer an employer. Part Two of *Your Career and Life Plan Portfolio*

- Describes the effect your career and life values and your learning and personality styles have on your career decisions

- Helps you define your self-management style—how you make decisions, take risks, manage your time, deal with stress, and stay physically and emotionally healthy

- Helps you understand your changing life roles and how they impact your career decisions

- Assists you in identifying careers that interest you most

- Guides you in describing the experience, skills, and education you have to offer an employer

- Provides help for dealing successfully with life changes

Part Three of this book will benefit you in setting and achieving career goals. As you complete the workbook, you will see that Part Three

- Helps you define the ideal job for you

- Assists you in identifying sources of career information and available training

- Describes the steps involved in making career decisions

- Explains how to evaluate and act on career information

- Guides you in preparing resumes and cover letters

- Provides details about contacting employers, interviewing and following up with employers, and evaluating job offers

- Includes information on being successful and growing in a new job

Using the Worksheets

This book provides numerous worksheets for you to complete. The pages are perforated and three-hole punched, so you can easily remove the worksheets if you choose.

Chapter 1 describes the various sections of a portfolio. You might want to put completed worksheets in those sections, wherever you think they would be relevant. Or you may choose to create a separate section of your portfolio for storing completed worksheets and other documents you want to have available as you look for a job.

Or you may decide not to remove the worksheets from the book. You could complete them and then keep the workbook handy for reference.

The worksheets ask you to fill in information, answer questions, or mark checklists. In some cases you may want to use additional sheets of paper. Also, remember that you can complete the worksheets more than once. You might respond to them as you work through the book for the first time and again at another stage of your career search.

Your replies to the worksheets can be as long or as short as you see fit. If you prefer, you can even draw pictures or diagrams instead of using words. You may also want to insert photographs or pictures from newspapers or magazines. Do whatever makes sense to you as you think about your life and work.

At the end of each section, you'll find a checklist of concepts and skills discussed in that chapter. Mark the items that reflect what you have learned. Then, go back through the chapter or seek out other resources to learn more about the items you could not check.

Getting Additional Help

If you get stuck or decide you need additional help with any of the steps in career planning, help is available in many forms. You can consult other books, people who work in careers that interest you, training programs and colleges of interest, professional associations, and the Internet (a good site to start with is www.jist.com). You may also wish to reach out to career counselors and advisors.

Career counselors, job trainers, and other professionals can be found in adult education programs, colleges and universities, community and government agencies, and the military. Many corporations and libraries employ career professionals. You may also want to contact professionals who are in private practice or who work in outplacement firms in your area.

Career professionals can test your occupational interests and make you aware of education and training possibilities. They can help you write resumes and prepare for interviews. They can teach you to match your skills to job possibilities and provide you with information about the labor market. They can offer advice on coping with career dissatisfaction, job loss, or job change.

You can locate career professionals by contacting your local adult education program, college, or university or by calling your local state employment service. You may want to visit your local library for information about professional associations. Also, look through the telephone directory for counselors in private practice or for community agencies that provide career or job-training services.

Consider contacting the National Board of Certified Counselors (NBCC) for a list of certified career counselors in your area.

> NBCC
> 3 Terrace Way, Suite D
> Greensboro, NC 27403-3660
> Phone number: 336-547-0607
> Web address: www.nbcc.org
> E-mail address: nbcc@nbcc.org

You can also contact the International Association of Counseling Services (AICS).

> AICS
> 101 S. Whiting Street, Suite 211
> Alexandria, VA 22304
> Phone number: 703-823-9840
> Web address: www.iacsinc.org
> E-mail address: iacs@gmu.edu

Congratulations to you for deciding to complete this workbook and invest in your future! Your preparation greatly increases your chance of finding success!

Part One

Creating a Portfolio

Chapter 1

Introduction to Portfolios

Welcome to the world of portfolios! The idea of creating a portfolio may be new to you. Or you may be familiar with the concept but just need a little extra help. You may even have a portfolio but feel that it could be improved. The information in this chapter will help you answer these questions:

- What is a portfolio?

- How can a portfolio benefit me?

- How do my goals affect my portfolio?

- What type of portfolio would work best for me?

- What kind of information should be included in my portfolio?

- How should my portfolio be organized?

- How can I display the information in my portfolio?

- How can I use my portfolio in job interviews?

Finding a job is hard work. Human resources professionals say that candidates who are prepared, organized, and focused have a definite edge over those who are not. A portfolio that is professionally organized and presented is a tool you can use to successfully demonstrate to the employer who you are and who you can be.

Definition of a Portfolio

A portfolio is a logically organized collection of records that reflects your accomplishments, skills, and attributes. It highlights your work and life experience. Also, a portfolio can help you and the job interviewer understand your career path and the steps you have taken to improve your work life. Your portfolio showcases your accomplishments and reflects your career goals and values. It also demonstrates the knowledge, skills, and preferences you have that will make you an asset to the employer.

> Your portfolio showcases your accomplishments and reflects your career goals and values.

The use of portfolios is not new. Artists, graphic artists, and teachers have long used portfolios. In fact, the term *portfolio* comes from the Italian word *portafoglio,* meaning *to carry leaves or sheets*. The term was used by artists during the Renaissance. Due to our changing work world, portfolios have become extremely helpful in modern life. Today, people in virtually every profession use portfolios as part of their job search.

Benefits of a Portfolio

Never have our work lives been so uncertain. There was a time when people could reasonably expect to get a good job and remain at one company for decades, eventually retiring with a reasonable level of security. No more! In today's global economy, events in distant corners of the world can and do have a profound impact on our ability to hold a good job. In the past, one set of skills and one company were the norm. Now we are faced with an ever-changing economy and job market. We must be able to transition into new careers, find new jobs, acquire new skills, and apply our existing skills to new uses.

> Creating a portfolio is a wonderful way to build your self-confidence. A portfolio carefully built over time accentuates the positive and reflects genuine growth and accomplishment.

The current buzzword is *self-direction,* which means that we must take control of our job search, determine our direction, and aggressively advance toward our goal. And, we must adopt new tools to help us present ourselves effectively. Gone forever are the days when a person could get a job by just filling out an application.

When you present yourself to prospective employers, you start off with a blank slate; and you are faced with the problem of how to present a positive, believable, and accurate picture of yourself. Creating and maintaining a career portfolio will help you do this. A portfolio provides a comprehensive record of your accomplishments and can help you achieve success in your job search. A portfolio is useful for every kind of job.

Also, creating a portfolio is a wonderful way to build your self-confidence. People tend to minimize their accomplishments and exaggerate their flaws. We can be our own worst critics. A portfolio carefully built over time accentuates the positive and reflects genuine growth and accomplishment.

Many people never take the time to thoroughly examine themselves, but knowing who you are and what you want in life helps you establish and achieve your goals. You can learn a lot about who you are by gathering information for your portfolio.

Responding to Changes in the Workplace

The world of work changes rapidly, and each of us is impacted. Recognizing and anticipating change ensures that you are armed and ready to meet the challenge. Your portfolio reflects the changes in your personal and work lives and provides a framework for managing your career. It can help you cope with change creatively and take away your feelings of helplessness.

> Your portfolio reflects the changes in your personal and work lives and provides a framework for managing your career.

The personal information in your portfolio reflects the ever-changing balance between your goals, ambition, knowledge, and life experiences. Your portfolio includes specific examples of your change and growth and can be a powerful tool for marketing yourself. The portfolio does not replace the traditional resume, but is a powerful complement.

Assessing Yourself and Your Skills

People who look at portfolios, such as human resources professionals, tend to prize them highly. The reason is that a portfolio is truly the most objective and positive assessment of attributes and accomplishments a person can offer. It reflects the opinions of others. Letters of reference, certificates of achievement, performance evaluations, newspaper or magazine articles reflecting community achievement, thank-you letters from people you have helped, and numerous other documents reflect third-party opinions of your accomplishments.

> Each item in your portfolio is evidence of the skills you have acquired, the knowledge you have gained, and the values and characteristics that define you.

Each item in your portfolio is evidence of the skills you have acquired, the knowledge you have gained, and the values and characteristics that define you. As such, they are truly powerful in creating a positive first impression, which is absolutely critical in the initial stages of a job search.

You know that your experiences and achievements have helped you develop the skills employers seek, but describing how everything fits together is difficult. You must convey your skills and experiences and demonstrate your capabilities clearly and objectively. Your portfolio helps you do that.

Demonstrating a Logical Progression

Your portfolio is not just a random file of accomplishments; it is an organized review of your personal and professional achievements and growth. The way you organize your portfolio should demonstrate your progress toward achieving a measurable goal.

When you show someone your portfolio, you explain what the entries represent and how they fit a pattern of personal and professional growth. This does not mean that your portfolio has to be organized chronologically. In fact, the more diverse your portfolio is, the less relevant a chronological progression will be. For example, your portfolio might start with a section on education and training, then continue with accomplishments and job history, then skills and attributes, then values, and so forth. Each section might be arranged chronologically. The point is that any way you decide to organize your portfolio is acceptable. What is critical is the logic behind the organization you choose.

> Your portfolio is not just a random file of accomplishments; it is an organized review of your personal and professional achievements and growth.

Portfolios and Goal-Setting

Tip
Set specific, attainable, measurable goals. Determine a time frame for each achievement level. Set goals that are realistic.

When you set goals, you set a destination for yourself that may be difficult to reach; but setting goals can propel you to achieve. The process is simple. Set specific, attainable, measurable goals. Determine a time frame for each achievement level. Set goals that are realistic. Also consider the scope of your goals. Are they long-range or short-range?

You may also want to set some goals that can never be reached but that will provide you with lifelong direction. For example, one of your goals might be to keep learning during your entire life. Or you might set a goal of being number one or being the best you can be. Short-term objectives that are met along the path can provide you with the strength and courage to continue pursuing your ultimate goals.

While the process of setting goals is simple, achieving them may not be. We all encounter obstacles and opportunities that force us to reevaluate our goals. This is not necessarily bad. Both obstacles and opportunities help us maintain personal growth and enable us to adapt to the changes and challenges of work and life.

The importance of setting goals before you create your portfolio cannot be overstated. Why? Because goal setting allows you to see the specific actions you need to take to achieve the goal. It helps you identify major obstacles, and it forces you to think about ways to deal with these obstacles.

Before you can determine your goals and objectives, you must assess your strengths, weaknesses, and values. You must determine what you want from your career, what your skills and abilities are, and what you want to accomplish. You need to understand the abilities and skills you have developed through work experience and training. You could think of these abilities and skills as a product you are marketing to the employer. They enable you to get results and add value to your work. After you assess your competencies and skills, you can create a plan to improve them. You can then determine realistic goals and objectives. You will learn more about setting goals in other chapters of this book.

Types of Portfolios

There are many approaches to creating a portfolio. In general, once you create your basic portfolio and use it in a variety of settings, you will see that it can be fine-tuned to achieve one or more specific objectives. You may find that you need more than one portfolio so each portfolio can be tailored to a specific purpose.

Although various professions call for differing degrees of portfolio specialization, all portfolios have common elements and fall into three general categories. The first type of portfolio is best used by people who have many years of experience; the second is useful for recent graduates, people returning to the workforce, or anyone with limited work experience. A third type of portfolio combines the first two into a more balanced or blended approach and is suitable for a person who is targeting a particular job.

> Employers are interested in anything tangible that helps them make a decision. When interviewing, choose portfolio examples that best describe what you wish to communicate. Provide information that is clear, relevant, and interesting.

Before reading about the various portfolio types, you should know a little about the interviewing process. Most managers have a general idea about the type of person they want. They are not interested in a long explanation of your life and career activities. They don't have the time. However, they are interested in anything tangible that helps them make a final decision. You must choose the examples that best describe what you wish to communicate. You must provide information that is clear, relevant, and interesting. Your choice of materials is very important.

The first type of portfolio will be particularly useful to you if you have many years of experience and a high level of expertise. It should include numerous examples of your job accomplishments and other information related to your work experiences. Examples could be published articles, technical projects, graphic or other types of art, and drafting samples. Often, especially in a tight economy, hiring managers are more interested in knowing what you have accomplished than they are in knowing you as an individual. This is particularly true in technical professions. Therefore, your portfolio should largely reflect your work achievements, including your professional awards.

The second type of portfolio is the one to use if you are just entering the job market. Because you have limited work experience, you must convince the interviewer that you are a person with potential. Evidence of your academic credentials, achievement awards, and other accomplishments can be critical in the interviewing process. This information can heavily influence employers who are more interested in hiring quality individuals than in hiring people with numerous professional accomplishments.

The third portfolio type works well for people who are targeting a particular job. It blends elements of the other two types. When you use this type of portfolio, you must be sure not to create an encyclopedia. Include only the examples and information that emphasize or clarify your goals. For example, if you apply for a position as an electronics technician or graphic artist, the fact that you won the Little League Coach-of-the-Year award, while interesting, would not be relevant to your career goal.

The Master Portfolio

Earlier we noted that although there is no standard way to organize a portfolio, it should be organized logically to reflect your goals and aspirations. Your portfolio must take into account the criteria of the career you seek. That means that you must understand the job description of the position you want. Also, you must modify your portfolio to emphasize the attributes most valued by the prospective employer.

For example, if a position calls for versatility, you should emphasize your broad training, multiple projects, and diverse accomplishments. If the job calls for a high degree of teamwork, successful examples of working with other people would be appropriate.

> Your portfolio must take into account the criteria of the career you seek.

Does this mean you have to create a new portfolio every time you have a job interview? Not at all! One frequently recommended approach is to create a master portfolio that contains all the elements discussed in this book. This is the complete record of all the important essentials of your background that you could use in any job search. Then, you would create another portfolio that is a subset of the master portfolio. It would include information relevant to a specific job search or interview.

Organizing Your Portfolio

The master portfolio is a living document. Update and refresh it often to ensure that your best accomplishments are captured and archived. Older material can be removed and discarded as appropriate.

Also, remember that one document may serve multiple purposes; for example, to show both experience and skills. Consider each category of information individually as you gather material for the portfolio. This will ensure completeness.

As you build your master portfolio, consider these seven categories:

- Personal Information
- Values
- Personal Goals and History
- Accomplishments and Job History
- Skills and Attributes
- Education and Training
- Testimonials and Recommendations

As you create your first portfolio, you will see that you have more materials than you need. Gathering as much information as possible allows you the flexibility of choosing the best examples and assigning the appropriate weight to each category.

Each of these categories will make up one section of your portfolio. As you create your first portfolio, you will see that you have more materials than you need. Gathering as much information as possible allows you the flexibility of choosing the best examples and assigning the appropriate weight to each category. Individual bits and pieces of information may not say much about you, but a bigger picture develops when you put the pieces together.

Also, consider making a separate section in your portfolio where you can file checklists and worksheets from this workbook. Include the ones you decide would be most helpful to have available. You can also include any other materials you choose.

Remember that the information in this extra section will be for your reference only. By including these items in your portfolio, you will have them available when you need the information they contain. You can also refer to these materials to be sure you are staying on track with your career and life plan.

If you do not want to put this book's worksheets in your portfolio, you could file it in a separate folder or notebook. Or you may decide to leave the worksheets in the workbook and just keep the book handy for when you need it.

Now let's look at the various sections of your portfolio.

Personal Information

> **Tip** Locating and gathering personal information may be the most time-consuming aspect of creating your portfolio, but it is also the most critical.

You may think that your personal information is just statistical data, but it can actually help you see yourself as other people see you. In this section of your portfolio, include the originals or copies of your

- Birth certificate
- Health records
- Picture identification or current photo
- Social Security card
- Passport
- Driver's license
- Work permit
- Noncitizen status papers
- Survey, test, or assessment results

Including copies of these documents in your portfolio ensures that you will have the information at your fingertips when you need it. If you wish to preserve your original documents in good condition, make photocopies of the originals and place copies in your portfolio.

Having a good sense of self helps you in all aspects of your life's work. Locating and gathering personal information may be the most time-consuming aspect of creating your portfolio, but it is also the most critical. You will be asked to provide this information every time you fill out a job application or interview for a job.

In addition to the items listed above, include the following worksheet in the Personal Information section of your portfolio. Employment laws vary from state to state, so you may not be asked to provide all of the information listed on the worksheet. However, you should be prepared to provide the information if asked.

My Personal Information

Full name _____

Other names I have used _____

Street address _____

City _____ State/Province _____ ZIP _____

Previous address _____

City _____ State/Province _____ ZIP _____

Telephone numbers: Home _____ Work _____

                      Pager _____ Cell phone _____

E-mail address _____

Mailing address (if different) _____

City _____ State/Province _____ ZIP _____

Social Security number _____

Driver's license number _____

Date of birth _____ Place of birth _____

U.S. citizen? (Y/N) _____ If not, current status _____

Visa _____ Registration number _____

Other: _____

_____

_____

Values

The Values section of a portfolio is the most difficult to define and document. However, with many corporations being scrutinized for unethical conduct, firms are now dusting off their corporate values statements and attempting to rejuvenate them. At the least, this means that human resources departments will be directed to ensure that new hires conform to corporate values. In general, these types of values statements encourage a cooperative working community based on trust and openness. They are meant to foster an atmosphere free of harassment and discrimination. They encourage a commitment to quality and integrity in the company's dealings with employees, vendors, and customers. Any examples in your work experience that reflect company values should be included.

> Your values define what you want from life, as an individual and as a worker. Clarifying your values will give you a sense of direction and purpose.

Your values reflect highly personal needs which you acquire from your family, education, social groups, and life experience. They are the basis of your motivation, interests, desires, and attitudes. Your values define what you want from life, as an individual and as a worker. Clarifying your values will give you a sense of direction and purpose, especially when you have the opportunity to select a new job or work environment.

As an employee, you will be the most content and productive in jobs that allow you to satisfy important values. Job dissatisfaction can easily result when your job does not satisfy your values; therefore, you should consider your values when you examine a work opportunity. Determine if the job is in line with your values.

This section is closely related to other sections of your portfolio. You can include the documentation either in this section or in one of the other sections. This would include documentation of your public and community service, your leadership and honesty, your church involvement, or your participation in various charitable organizations. Your involvements indicate what your values are.

Personal Goals and History

Generally placed at the beginning of a portfolio, this is a short section describing your career goals and objectives. It is a good place to comment on your career progression. It provides an opportunity for reflective input and personal history. As you review the other sections of your portfolio with an interviewer, point out the connections between those sections and the Personal Goals and History section. This is an excellent way to emphasize your commitment and consistency to a career direction. Your explanation will be appreciated by human resources personnel.

> Personal Goals and History is a short section describing your career goals and objectives. It is a good place to comment on your career progression.

Accomplishments and Job History

Even though each section of your portfolio is important, your accomplishments and job history are clearly the most important. This is a good place for your resume (more information on resumes in Chapter 7). This section should include a chronological listing of employment. It should describe job-related accomplishments clearly and should include both paid and unpaid work experience. Relevant information for each job includes a complete job description, the organization's

> The Job History section is a chronological listing of employment. It should describe job-related accomplishments clearly and should include both paid and unpaid work experience.

address, your supervisor's name, and your performance evaluations. References and letters of commendation are extremely helpful in reinforcing the information. Finally, visual representations are extremely important. One picture is definitely worth a thousand words; therefore, artwork, photos, graphs, graphics, designs, articles, or any other visual aids that reinforce your message should be included.

Skills and Attributes

You may acquire skills through formal or informal training or on the job. Any skill that relates to a specific position should be clearly identified; for example, technical, computer, industrial, or mechanical skills.

Special knowledge that is unique to a profession can also be considered a skill. For example, you may have an understanding of financial documents, contracts, healthcare regulations, or market research processes. These contribute to your overall skill set, so be sure to include them in your portfolio. In many cases, what you know can be even more important than what you have done.

> If you have acquired special skills or knowledge from a hobby or something that interests you, your portfolio should reflect this.

Also, if you have acquired special skills or knowledge from a hobby or something that interests you, your portfolio should also reflect this.

Attributes are intangible qualities and may be difficult to quantify. They can often make the difference between success and failure. Some examples of attributes that lead to success are the ability to communicate effectively, to work in a team setting, to learn quickly, to follow instructions, to accept criticism gracefully, and to be creative. Any documents or information you have that demonstrates these attributes should be part of your portfolio.

One oddity in the hiring and interviewing process is that many firms assume that if a person had a skill in the past, he still has that skill. The employer assumes not only that the person can perform but that he can perform well. As a result, the hiring decision is often based more on the candidate's attributes than on his skills.

Education and Training

A complete education and training record should be included in this section of your portfolio. Course descriptions, transcripts, and practical examples of completed projects can be very helpful. Documents of achievement from seminars, workshops, and professional development courses should also be considered for inclusion. If you are just entering the workforce or have limited experience, invest some careful thought and planning in this section. If you have significant work experience, you will not have to spend as much time on this section, but your academic achievements still should be included.

> The idea of lifelong learning has gained importance over the years. It refers to the efforts you make to continue learning even after you have finished your formal schooling.

One category of learning you should consider is experiential learning. This is learning you gain through life experiences, and it cannot be easily categorized. It is often, but not always, gained on the job. The idea of lifelong learning has gained importance over the years. It refers to the efforts you make to continue learning even after you have finished your formal schooling. Include examples of lifelong learning in your portfolio. By doing so, you show that you are committed to change, which is so much a part of today's work world. Address all the skills and capabilities you have learned through nontraditional methods.

Testimonials and Recommendations

Any form of positive assessment or job reference should be included in your portfolio. A good assessment is one that is specific. You should show how the skills and attributes described in the assessment relate to the achievements included in other sections of your portfolio. Your portfolio will be more credible if you can show how an acknowledged skill or attribute is demonstrated over and over in subsequent performance.

> Your portfolio will be more credible if you can show how an acknowledged skill or attribute is demonstrated over and over in subsequent performance.

Awards and certificates that demonstrate achievement in unrelated fields should also be included in this section of your portfolio. Examples include honors conferred through membership in organizations or through volunteer and community involvement. These honors show your professionalism, cooperation, and team spirit.

Displaying Your Portfolio

The following information refers only to paper-based portfolios. The key point regarding presentation can be summed up in one word—*professionalism*. No matter how impressive or exciting the content of your portfolio may be, it will not be as effective as it could be if it does not have a professional look and feel.

Original documents should be included wherever possible, with each item enclosed in its own transparent plastic cover. You may be concerned about maintaining certain original documents in good condition. If so, you can include clean, clear copies instead. The copies should be free of random marks.

> No matter how impressive or exciting the content of your portfolio may be, it will not be as effective as it could be if it does not have a professional look and feel. Your ability to present your material professionally can give you an edge in the job search process.

Separators and labels should divide each section of your portfolio, and the labels should be typed. You can use a large artist-type cover, but most people use a three-ring binder. Include a cover sheet on the front of the binder, noting that this is a portfolio and giving your name, address, e-mail address, and telephone number. Be sure the size of the binder is consistent with the volume of material. The binder should not look empty, but it should also not look stuffed.

During an interview, you may want to have the items loosely placed in a briefcase so you can pull them out as you need them. Ideally, you will have a few minutes to present your whole portfolio. Emphasize entries you believe will strengthen your interview.

Graphs, pictures, drawings, blueprints, designs, and any other visual aids should look appealing and should be in color, if possible. Handle the portfolio carefully. Remove any smudges or handprints.

Remember that in addition to subject matter, appearance can make a difference. Your ability to present your material professionally can give you an edge in the job search process.

Portfolios and Job Interviews

After you have collected the material that will be included in your portfolio, you are ready to think about how you will present the information to employers. Remember that, to the untrained eye, one portfolio entry carries as much weight as any other. A quick review of the contents does not tell the interviewer what you can do for the company. In fact, the parts of your portfolio that relate to the position you are applying for may be spread across several entries.

Before the Interview

You must be able to talk about your portfolio examples as you show them to an employer. Getting ready to do this requires three things: preparation, preparation, and preparation.

Identify items in your portfolio that show that you have skills and achievements that are directly related to the job you want. Think about how you could describe each skill or achievement to an employer. You can think of these descriptions as short stories. Practice saying them aloud. No description should last more than 1½ minutes. In each story, describe your skill or accomplishment, the actual problem or need you faced, the action you took to solve the problem or meet the need, and the results. Remember that you want to convince the employer that you can do the job.

As you decide which portfolio examples to present to an employer, consider all your accomplishments—even those you did not have to work hard to achieve. An interviewer might be impressed by an accomplishment that does not seem important to you. Being modest at an interview is not a virtue.

> You must be able to talk about your portfolio examples as you show them to an employer. Being modest at an interview is not a virtue.

During the Interview

When you present your portfolio to an employer, focus on information that relates to the job you want. Point out examples that demonstrate your experience, accomplishments, and training. If you can describe your successes clearly, your job search may be shortened. People want to help a candidate they believe is qualified for a job.

Employers want to know that you can apply your skills and achievements to their organization's problems and needs. Use your portfolio examples to reinforce your descriptions of your achievements. You gain credibility with the employer when you are able to both describe and show examples of what you have done and what you can do.

> You gain credibility with the employer when you are able to both describe and show examples of what you have done and what you can do.

At the end of the interview, if you are interested in the job, express your interest to the employer. Briefly describe why you want the job. Emphasize how your specific skills and accomplishments would fit the job. Then ask the interviewer if he or she has any concerns about your ability to do the job. Consider the feedback you receive and address any issues the employer raises.

▶*LET'S REVIEW*

Complete the following worksheet. Review information in this chapter that applies to any items you are unable to check.

Self-Assessment Checklist

_____ I know the various portfolio types, and I can explain which type would work best for me.

_____ I have thought about what items to include in the Personal Information section of my portfolio.

_____ I know one thing I want to include in the Values section of my portfolio.

_____ I know one item I want to include in the Personal Goals and History section.

_____ I know one piece of documentation I want to include in the Accomplishments and Job History section of my portfolio.

_____ I can describe one item I could include in the Skills and Attributes section.

_____ I have thought of one item I want to include in the Education and Training section of my portfolio.

_____ I know one item to include in the Testimonials and Recommendations section.

Date:_____

Chapter 2

Portfolio Organization

Now that you have been introduced to portfolios, you are ready for some specifics. This chapter will help you answer these questions:

- How do I decide what to include in my portfolio?
- How should I arrange the various sections of my portfolio?
- Do I need an electronic portfolio?
- How do I create a CD?
- How do I create a Web site?
- What are some things I should or should not do when preparing my portfolio?

This book introduces you to a set of tools that can help you succeed. But they are only tools. Hopefully, this book will inspire you to build on your skills and to manage your professional life proactively.

The Process

As noted in the previous chapter, there is no standard way of organizing a portfolio. What is important is to organize your portfolio in a way that seems logical for your situation. Start with a set of goals and objectives, and keep in mind that employers are looking for both skills and attributes that fit their needs.

> Think of your portfolio as a marketing tool—and you are what is being marketed. Evaluate yourself objectively, understand your strengths and weaknesses, and develop a set of meaningful goals.

You can think of your portfolio as a marketing tool—and *you* are what is being marketed. You must evaluate yourself objectively, understand your strengths and weaknesses, and develop a set of meaningful goals. You must also seek out potential employers whose needs fit your skills. (Chapters 5 and 6 will give you more information about identifying potential employers.)

The creation and development of your portfolio is a complex process. It requires self-reflection, critical and honest self-assessment, and just plain hard work. Melding all your experience, education, goals, and objectives into a logically flowing and visually pleasing career tool is definitely a challenge. And creating the portfolio is just the beginning.

As mentioned in Chapter 1, a portfolio is a living document. It must be updated, reshaped, and modified as you proceed along your career path. The more experience you gain, the more employers will expect from you. You must show them that you can meet their expectations. Your portfolio can help you do that.

Creating your portfolio can be a rewarding experience. The portfolio requires you to take a close look at where you have been, where you are now, and where you want to be. Creating a portfolio can empower you to take control of your career. Career development is an ongoing process, not a one-time event. You must be able to make the decisions that will help you reach your career goals. The portfolio is a tool that can help make this possible.

Getting Started

Start developing your portfolio by taking a personal inventory. Review your professional competencies and skills, your personal strengths, and your personal and professional goals and priorities. Follow these steps:

> Define yourself. Define your opportunities. Define a strategy. Define your approach.

- Define yourself. List your credentials, skills, knowledge, interests, strengths, and weaknesses.

- Define your opportunities. List competencies you have that are most needed by employers, types of organizations that appeal to you most, and management styles that are most comfortable for you.

- Define a strategy. Focus on a certain job or career.

- Define your approach. Determine how you will present yourself and your main message and what you will do to create a good first impression.

If this is the first time you have articulated your strengths, capabilities, intentions, and professional goals, do so carefully and thoroughly. As you are assembling and collecting items you could include in your portfolio, a logical pattern will begin to emerge. Following this pattern will enable you to develop a meaningful portfolio that is a true reflection of who you are. When you are finished, you will have the foundation of your job search strategy.

Be aware that many occupations are represented by organizations that set standards for their members. These organizations describe what people in a certain occupation should be able to do and how they should conduct their business. The groups also help members set goals for improving their skills and determine a realistic time frame for reaching those goals.

Look for organizations that might be available to people in your profession. This will help you understand what will be expected from you. It will help you set goals for developing skills you don't currently have. In your portfolio, include information about your membership in these kinds of organizations. For specific organizations that relate to your career goals, check out the following Web site— http://info.asaenet.org/gateway/onlineassocslist.html.

Choosing and Evaluating Content

Tip Use your self-assessment and goals to determine which items fit your portfolio best.

In Chapter 1, we reviewed the categories of material that should be collected. Now you have to choose what is the best material in each category, based on the goals you have set. For example, if your goal is to find a position involving leadership or decision making, choose items that refer to your past leadership responsibilities. You can include experiences that are not work related, such as serving as chairperson of your local youth soccer league. If you are technically proficient and want to pursue a technical career, anything referring to technical skills is good material. The point is that you should use your self-assessment and goals to determine which items fit your portfolio best.

The examples in the following worksheet will not necessarily match your interests, but they will give you an opportunity to practice matching goals and self-assessment to items that would be appropriate to include in a portfolio. Mark each item true or false and then briefly explain your answer.

I Choose and Evaluate Content

If my goal is to work with children: In the Values section of my portfolio, I could include the thank-you note I received from an elementary-school principal after I helped tutor two special needs children.   T____   F____

Explanation: _____

_____

If I am interested in a career in auto mechanics: In the Skills and Attributes section of my portfolio, I probably would <u>not</u> need to include the thank-you note from the school principal.   T____   F____

Explanation: _____

_____

If I want to enroll in a training program for paralegals: In the Education and Training section of my portfolio, I would want to include a copy of the certificate showing I was on the Honors Roll my last two semesters of high school.   T____   F____

Explanation: _____

_____

Building the Portfolio

Now you are ready to build your portfolio. You can arrange the various sections in any order, but remember that the goal is to use the portfolio to get a job. You should begin with a simple table of contents that identifies the sections of the portfolio. A suggested flow for your portfolio is

1. Values

2. Personal Goals and History

3. Accomplishments and Job History

4. Skills and Attributes

5. Education and Training

6. Testimonials and Recommendations

Content and presentation are far more important than the order of the sections in your portfolio. Remember that the goal is to use the portfolio to get a job.

The order suggested here is appropriate for the typical job seeker. Remember that content and presentation are far more important than the order of the sections in your portfolio.

The Values section and the Personal Goals and History section should be short unless you have something especially unusual and significant to say. The more work experience you have, the more emphasis you should give to the Accomplishments and Job History section.

Measuring the Results

Tip Ask other people to look at your portfolio and tell you whether they think the goals you set are truly reflected in the portfolio.

Your assessment of your final portfolio is subjective. However, reviewing your portfolio is a good way to see if the contents are properly focused. It also gives you an opportunity to think about whether your planned career path is really right for you. You may decide you should choose another path and head in a different direction. If you are content with your direction, focus on the portfolio as a vehicle for achieving success.

Before using your portfolio in job interviews, review it to be sure it says what you want it to say. Then ask other people to look at your portfolio and tell you whether they think the goals you set are truly reflected in the portfolio. After a job interview, think about whether the portfolio items you used were effective.

Electronic Portfolios

The question of whether to go electronic is fast becoming a "no-brainer." We are approaching the day when people will not be considered for employment if they do not have some sort of electronic presence, such as a Web site. This is especially true for people in creative professions. It is also true for people working in any business that uses technology in the normal course of its work. People in these businesses are expected to have computer proficiency even if their jobs do not specifically require it.

> We are approaching the day when people will not be considered for employment if they do not have some sort of electronic presence, such as a Web site.

You will at least want to have an electronic version of your resume that can be e-mailed to employers. You may also want to scan other portfolio documents to create electronic files that can be e-mailed.

A Cautionary Note

Electronic media are all the rage. People commonly put their portfolios on CD's (compact discs) or send the documents by e-mail. Personal Web sites are everywhere. The natural assumption is that these media will soon overtake and totally replace hardcopy versions of the portfolio, but that assumption is incorrect. Why? Recruiters and human resources personnel do not have time to consider all the information you could include on a CD or a Web site. They do not even have time to look at all the resumes they receive.

> No matter how well organized your electronic portfolio is, an employer may view it as simply a set of random documents. However, when you present your hardcopy portfolio in an interview, you can put each item in context.

No matter how well organized your electronic portfolio is, an employer may view it as simply a set of random documents. However, when you present your hardcopy portfolio in an interview, you can put each item in context. Each entry emphasizes and validates the points you wish to communicate.

Although the process of screening candidates is relatively mechanical, the interviewing process is not. It is an intensely human encounter, where the parties have an opportunity to meet face to face, size each other up, and make a determination as to suitability. In this context, the hardcopy version of your portfolio is most effective.

Computer-assisted interviewing does take place in professions that employ large numbers of people, such as telemarketing, hotel management, and retail sales. Time alone will tell whether this practice represents a fundamental change or is only a trend.

The Role of Electronic Portfolios

Even though you should not abandon your hardcopy portfolio, you should consider developing an electronic version of your portfolio also. Why? Electronic portfolios are a relatively inexpensive way to market yourself in a substantive way. You can use your portfolio to reach a lot of people in a short time. You can distribute information about yourself to employers who would not otherwise know who you are.

Although employers will spend little time viewing your CD or Web site and not read it in detail, it can create a positive impression. People are just beginning to use Web portfolios, so recruiters or human resources people might stop to look at your portfolio carefully if it includes items that catch their eye. This won't get you a job, but it might get you an interview.

> Electronic portfolios are a relatively inexpensive way to market yourself in a substantive way. You can use your portfolio to reach a lot of people in a short time. You can distribute information about yourself to employers who would not otherwise know who you are.

A Web-based portfolio can be a convenient way to update your current job accomplishments as you prepare for the next job, promotion, or raise. It also facilitates long-distance networking and can be helpful in situations where a two-dimensional presentation is inadequate. A video or audio representation can demonstrate a skill or accomplishment that is important to an employer.

Generally, the philosophy and contents of an electronic portfolio mirror those of the paper version. However, keep in mind that you can select the material you will show in an interview, but you cannot select what material an employer will choose to view or not view on your Web site or CD. For this reason, you must be particularly careful what you include. One thing you must include is a text version of your resume.

The electronic portfolio can be an exciting new tool to help in the job search and should not be overlooked. The more technically proficient you are, the more opportunity you have to be creative. For example, simple text documents can be enhanced in marvelous ways through software programs such as Microsoft PowerPoint. Graphics software such as Adobe Photoshop can add color, design, emphasis, and special effects.

To create a CD or Web site, you must be able to access the necessary information and utilize the available tools. This requires at least a basic level of technology skill. The good news is that even a beginner can learn to create electronic documents fairly quickly.

Creating a CD

A portfolio on a CD is fixed and permanent and is not easily updated. But you can easily mail or give your CD to employers.

Creating a Web Site

Unlike your portfolio on CD, your Web site can and should be modified often. Web sites are interactive information sources with links that enable communication to other resources.

Designing a Web site is not difficult or expensive, but it does require some artistic flair. Inexpensive, easy-to-use software is now available to help you to achieve a look that communicates a message.

> Web sites are interactive information sources with links that enable communication to other resources. Your Web site can and should be modified often.

Almost as soon as someone prints a list of available software and costs, the list is obsolete. New tools that are easier to use and that cost less are constantly being introduced. This is certainly true of Web site software. You could spend $1,000 or more to hire a professional to create your Web site, but let's assume you do not want to do that. To create your own electronic portfolio, you need three things:

1. **You need Web-creation software.** Software for beginners is available for as little as $50. This software will walk you through the process of building a Web site, tell you how to register with a Web hosting service (usually their own), and get you started online. If you are artistic, you can create an impressive Web site with low-cost software.

   For information about software, search the Web with the keywords *Web Site Software.*

2. **You need a domain name or URL (Uniform Resource Locator).** Technically, the terms *domain name* and *URL* have different definitions, but they are often used interchangeably. Your domain name is your Web address. For information about registering a domain name, simply enter the keywords *Domain Name* and you will find sources and instructions for registering.

   You might choose a name such as www.harrysgreatportfolio.com or www.hiresuzy.org. You can make up any name or combination of names, check online for availability, and register the name with one of the online domain name services. Current costs are about $50 for three years. You must renew the name or you can lose it. The services will remind you when it is time to renew.

3. **You need a Web hosting service.** This is the organization that will maintain your Web site, create an e-mail mailbox, and provide you with a range of services. Prices currently range from $10 per month (which basically leaves you on your own) to $25 per month (which provides you with real technical help).

You can get information about these services by searching the Web with the keywords *Web Hosting Services.*

Numerous Web sites are available to help you create your online portfolio. The list below is by no means complete, but it does represent a cross section of the information that is available:

www.rit.edu (Keyword: Portfolio)

amby.com/kimeldorf

www.ash.udel.edu

transition.Alaska.edu/www/portfolios.html

electronicportfolios.com

www.quintcareers.com/career_portfolios.html

www.wa.gov/esd/lmea/soicc/prtfolio.htm

www.datasync.com/~teachers/portfolio.html

www.bsu.edu/students/careers/documents/portfoli/

You already have tools on your computer that let you check for the compactness of your graphics. Put your cursor on the graphic image and right click the mouse. Look down the screen that pops up and you will see a line that says "properties." Click that and it will tell you how many bytes your graphic takes up. Your Web hosting service will have software that will maintain the graphic's integrity but compact it so that it takes up fewer bytes and downloads faster.

Some Dos and Don'ts

- **Do** give out your Web address. It is as important as your name or telephone number and should be listed on your resume, business card, and correspondence. When you give out your telephone number verbally, you should also give your Web address.

- **Do** limit the amount of information you put on the Web site. Content is key. You will not have an opportunity for explanations, except for some introductory text. Consequently, the Web content must be carefully chosen and professionally presented.

- **Do** update your Web site frequently. Web flexibility is important, so you must be able to make routine changes to the site. You can buy inexpensive software that lets you do virtually anything. Your hosting service can also help.

- **Do** aim for compactness. You want prospective employers to be able to download the Web site quickly. Avoid using fancy, space-eating graphics.

- **Do** include information about how employers can contact you by telephone, fax, and e-mail.

- **Do** take a look at other Web sites and ask your friends and colleagues for suggestions. Have at least one person look at your Web site before you go live.

- **Do** use color copies of your Web site if you don't use a hardcopy portfolio. Refer to Chapter 1 for suggestions on presenting your portfolio in an interview.

- **Do** keep your Web site clean, simple, and honest.

- **Don't** indicate on your Web site that you are looking for work. Be discrete. You don't want your current employer to suspect the reason behind your electronic portfolio.

- **Don't** spam. The term *spam* refers to unsolicited e-mail. Target your electronic portfolio to a carefully chosen audience that matches your career search parameters.

- **Don't** put your picture on your Web site. You want to avoid any issues relative to employment laws.

- **Don't** get flashy. Don't use blinking lights, pop-up screens, fancy fonts, or other gimmicks.

- **Don't** include too much personal information. Be cautious. Remember that anyone can view your online portfolio.

The Importance of the Internet

Chapter 1 began with a brief description of the new world-of-work and defined the term *self-direction*. Today's job market requires preparation and flexibility. Lifelong learning is a must for workers who want to expand their opportunities. In addition, we must be communicators and marketers, and we must be able to sell an employer on our credentials and potential.

So how can we cope? Jobs come and go. Companies start up and then fold. Decisions in places far from us have a profound influence on our jobs. Why bother using the Internet?

> Today's job market requires preparation and flexibility.

Using the Internet can help you cope with the changing job market. It provides information that was not previously available and can be used as a vehicle for searching for worldwide opportunities. You can communicate with employers electronically to find a new career in a new location. The Internet levels the playing field significantly for people who would not otherwise have the resources to search for job opportunities in other locations.

We sometimes feel helpless in coping with outside forces, but the Internet has connected all of us in new and exciting ways. It has opened doors and revealed some amazing opportunities. You can use the Internet to respond substantively to change and to unforeseen, negative shifts in your work environment. The key is to be committed and to reposition yourself and your career aspirations over time.

▶*LET'S REVIEW*

Complete the following worksheet. Review information in this chapter that applies to any items you are unable to check.

Self-Assessment Checklist

_____ I know how to choose and evaluate documents to be included in my portfolio.

_____ I know of one or more people I can ask to review my portfolio.

_____ I can describe what an electronic portfolio is.

_____ I am considering creating a portfolio CD.

_____ I understand the basics of creating a Web site.

_____ I know where to find online support for creating my Web site.

_____ I can name some of the dos and don'ts of creating an electronic portfolio.

_____ I plan to create my own Web site.

Date: _____

Part Two

Understanding Yourself

Chapter 3

Who You Are

As you build, organize, and use your portfolio, you will need to understand who you are. You have interests, abilities, and values that make you unique. Gathering information about yourself is a first step on the road to a satisfying occupation. This chapter will help you answer these questions:

- What do I value in my life and career?

- What are my learning and personality styles?

- What self-management skills do I need for making decisions, taking risks, managing my time, dealing with stress, staying healthy, and finding emotional support?

- What are my past, current, and future roles in life and how do these affect my career decisions?

- What kind of work am I most interested in doing?

Knowing the answers to these questions can help you cope with job change, choose a new career direction, and persuade employers to hire you.

You may want to include the worksheets in this chapter in your portfolio. They can be placed in the Values section or in the Personal Goals and History section, or in any other section you think is appropriate. Most of these worksheets are not intended to be shown to employers, but they can serve as valuable references for you. They will help you build and organize your portfolio and consider career options.

Values

Many people believe that who you are is a reflection of what you value. Your values motivate you, both in your work and in your life, and each of us has his own ideas about what's important. If you can balance what's important in your life with what's important in your work, you will find satisfaction both on and off the job.

> After you talk to an employer and interview for a job, compare your list of values to what the job can offer you.

You may not find many career options that match all of your career and life values. However, for an occupation to be satisfying, it should fulfill many of your important values.

As you explore various career options, match what you have learned about your values to the descriptions of the occupations. After you talk to an employer and interview for a job, you can compare your list of values to what the job can offer you.

Career Values

If you value the work you do, you are more committed to working and to doing the job. Here are a few examples of work values:

> If you value the work you do, you are more committed to working and to doing the job.

- Income level
- Safety
- Work environment
- Skills development
- Teamwork
- Change and variety
- Independence
- Creativity
- Competition
- Advancement
- Structure and security
- Physical challenges
- Helping others
- Taking risks

If you have difficulty identifying what you value, talk with close friends or family members. They may be able to give you some insight. Self-assessment instruments can also help you discover more about your values. Several types of self-scoring instruments, including computerized assessment systems, may be available at your nearby high school, adult education center, college, or university. Most are available free or for a small fee.

The following worksheet will help you think about what your career values are. Place check marks in one of the three columns to show how significant each career value is to you.

My Career Values

	Essential	Significant	Insignificant
Accomplishment			
Authority			
Belonging			
Challenge			
Competition			
Contribution			
Creativity			
Flexibility			
Income			
Independence			
Influence			
Order			
Peace of mind			
Power			
Prestige			
Recognition			
Responsibility			
Security			
Service to others			
Structure			
Variety			

Life Values

You've thought about what is important to you in your career. Now think about those things that are important to you outside of work. Here are a few examples of life values:

- Leisure time

- Family

- Hobbies or sports

- Friendships

- Community activities

- Religious activities

One way to understand your life values is to think about unpleasant experiences you would like to avoid in the future. For example, the death of a close family member may make you realize that life is short. If so, you may value family time. You could also think about your life values by recalling happy experiences you have had.

On the following worksheet, create a list of your ten most-important life values. Then, number the values in order of their importance to you. Share the list with people who know you well. Ask them if it matches what they know about you. Be sure your list reflects what *you* think is important, not what *others* say should be important.

My Life Values

Here's a list of the ten life values that are most important to me. I've numbered them to show the order of their importance.

_____   _____

_____   _____

_____   _____

_____   _____

_____   _____

_____   _____

_____   _____

_____   _____

_____   _____

_____   _____

Learning Styles

In Chapter 4 of this book, you will have an opportunity to think about the skills you have now and the skills you want to develop. To learn new skills more easily, you should first determine your personal learning style. The term *learning style* simply means *the way you learn.*

People learn in different ways, so understanding your personal learning style is vitally important.

Most people believe that learning and education are the same and that they come primarily, if not exclusively, from going to school. But that's simply not true. Take a look at the difference between education and learning in your own life. You are a student for only a few years but a learner for a lifetime. And, for most of us, the transition from student to self-directed learner is difficult. We must work to develop a learning style that is appropriately balanced between traditional and experiential learning.

People learn in different ways, so understanding your personal learning style is vitally important. The two basic types of learning are traditional learning and experiential learning:

1. Some of us learn best by reading books, listening to lectures, and participating in activities led by a teacher or instructor. This type of learning is called **traditional learning.** It is also sometimes referred to as classroom learning.

2. Others of us prefer to learn by doing something, by practicing, or by experimenting on our own. This is called **experiential learning.**

Of course, all of us learn in both ways, but you will have one way that you prefer or that helps you learn best. You should find out what is the right combination of learning styles for you. If you know what kind of learner you are and if you assume full and active responsibility for your learning, you will greatly magnify your chances for career success.

You should start by using a self-scoring inventory such as the *Kolb Learning Style Inventory* (LSI). Include in your portfolio the results of any tests you take.

After you know what kind of learner you are, you may want to make some adjustments. For example, if you find that you are very much a traditional learner, you may want to consider trying to learn something by just doing it, instead of by reading a book or watching a video about it.

Employers often express reservations about people who are strongly traditional or strongly experiential. Enhancing your learning style is a way to address an employer's concerns. The complaint against traditional learners is that they know a lot about theory but are often ineffective at applying the theory. The complaint about experiential learners is that they may be able to do something in one particular setting but are often not able to perform in unfamiliar settings. They don't understand the theory behind what they are doing, so they are unable to tell other people how to do it.

You must work to define your style, find the right balance between traditional and experiential learning, and make any necessary adjustments.

Personality Styles

We have seen that understanding your learning style is a factor in developing new skills. Another important factor is your personality style. Numerous personality tests and checklists are available to help you. Be sure to choose a test that provides information related to career choices. Include in your portfolio the results of any tests you take.

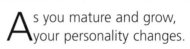
As you mature and grow, your personality changes.

The following chart gives some examples of how your personality impacts your selection of a career.

If you like...	Do not select an occupation in which...
Change and variety in your work	You do the same tasks day after day
Meeting and talking with new people	You work alone in an office
Planning your activities	You have constant interruptions

33

When you review your personality style, you may discover areas you would like to develop more fully. As you mature and grow, your personality changes. Use the following worksheet to begin thinking about your personality style.

My Personality Style

Two ways to describe my behavior at work are

1. _____

2. _____

Two ways to describe my behavior at home are

1. _____

2. _____

Two ways I react to work situations are

1. _____

2. _____

Two ways I react to life situations are

1. _____

2. _____

I would describe my personality or temperament as _____

_____

_____

People who have known me for a long time would describe my personality as _____

_____

_____

People who have met me only once would describe my personality as _____

_____

_____

Self-Management Styles

Self-management style is a term used to describe the way you handle life. It refers to

- Making decisions

- Taking risks

- Managing your time

- Dealing with stress

- Staying healthy

- Finding emotional support

> If you aren't entirely satisfied with how you handle circumstances and events in your life, you're not alone. The good news is that self-management skills can be learned.

These aspects of your self-management style are interrelated. Understanding your self-management style is important when you are choosing a career direction, making a career transition, or talking to a prospective employer.

The worksheets on the following pages will help you determine if your self-management style is working for you. If you aren't entirely satisfied with how you handle circumstances and events in your life, you're not alone. The good news is that self-management skills can be learned.

If your current strategies aren't working, think about trying some new ones. Talk with people you admire. Ask them about their self-management styles. Visit your local library or bookstore to find resources that relate to managing life.

Managing your personal life makes it easier to manage your career. You need a self-management style that helps you achieve good results in all areas of your life.

Making Decisions

How do you usually make decisions? This is one aspect of your self-management style. Here are some guidelines for effective decision making:

- Define the problem. State the underlying problem, not the surface problem. Be specific. State the problem as a question.

- State the goal. Clearly describe the outcomes you want.

- List alternative solutions. Determine which are safe and which require risk. List possible outcomes of each solution.

- Collect information. Expand your list of alternatives. Describe the kind of information you need and where you can obtain it. Decide if the information is relevant to the problem.

> Define the problem. State the goal. List alternative solutions. Collect information. Compare several alternatives. Choose one alternative. Take action on your choice. Review your choice. Make new decisions.

- Compare several alternatives with what you know about your values, your commitments to other people, your resources, and your constraints.

- Choose one alternative that is consistent with your stated goal.

- Take action on your choice. Determine how you will implement your choice. Decide what actions you can take now and later.

- Review your choice periodically.

- Make new decisions as your situation changes.

You may want to add this list of decision-making guidelines to your portfolio and refer to it when you are considering career and life changes.

Taking Risks

Making decisions and taking risks are closely related. All decisions involve some level of risk, and your risk-taking style influences your decisions. Here are five approaches to taking risks and making decisions:

> All decisions involve some level of risk, and your risk-taking style influences your decisions.

- The Wish Approach—The most important thing is to reach the desired outcome. Ignores risks.

- The Safe Approach—The most important thing is to not fail. Chooses the outcome with the highest probability of success.

- The Escape Approach—Chooses no outcome.

- The High-Risk Approach—The most important thing is to take a risk. Chooses the outcome that is most likely to fail.

- The Combination Approach—Risks and outcomes are both important. Balances a highly desirable outcome with a calculated risk.

For some people, changing occupations, starting a training program, getting more education, or looking for work may be exciting. For others, these activities may feel risky and may cause anxiety. As you think about your risk-taking style, consider the following:

- How much risk can I handle right now? How much risk do I want to handle in my career? In my next job?

- Do some things seem risky just because I don't know much about them?

- Do I know someone who has been faced with this kind of risk? Can I talk to that person?

- How will I benefit from change? Is the benefit worth the risk? What will happen if I don't take this chance?

- What can I do to make the change less risky?

- Who can give me support and encourage me?

The following worksheet can help you understand your risk-taking style more clearly.

My Risk-Taking Style

I remember times in my life when I was faced with several changes at once or with a life-changing decision.

I was comfortable with the change.   Yes_____   No_____

The decision came easily.   Yes_____   No_____

Two risks I've taken:_____

_____

_____

What motivated me to take the risks: _____

_____

_____

How my perception of the risks affected my decision:

1. _____

_____

_____

_____

2. _____

_____

_____

_____

Other risks I've taken in my life and career are   _____

_____

_____

I would describe my risk-taking style as _____

_____

_____

Managing Time

Planning a new career direction, exploring different occupations, and looking for work all require extra time and energy. For many of us, the time must be carved out of an already busy schedule. How well you manage your time definitely affects career planning and your performance on the job. Here are some questions you may want to consider:

How well you manage your time affects both your career planning and your performance on the job.

- Am I satisfied with how I manage my time both on and off the job? If not, how can I improve my time-management skills?

- What gets in the way of my accomplishing what is important to me?

- Do I spend enough time on my high-priority activities?

If you are not satisfied with how you manage your time, meet deadlines, or accomplish your goals, there are many books and tapes available on these topics. Ask your local librarian for suggestions. The following worksheet can help you get started evaluating and understanding your time-management style.

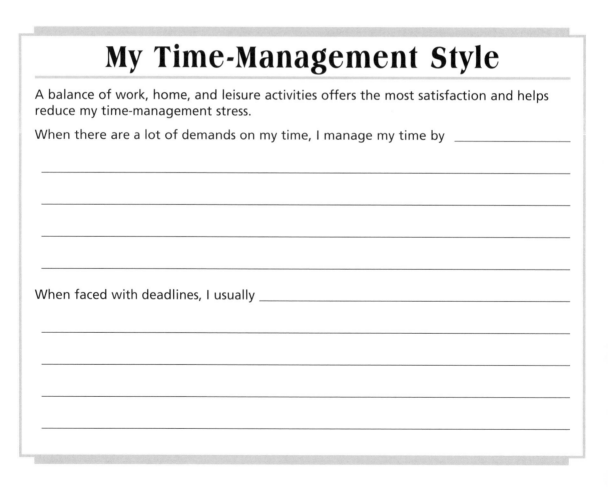

My Time-Management Style

A balance of work, home, and leisure activities offers the most satisfaction and helps reduce my time-management stress.

When there are a lot of demands on my time, I manage my time by _____

_____

_____

_____

_____

When faced with deadlines, I usually _____

_____

_____

_____

_____

Dealing with Stress

 Tip Exercise your mind and body to relieve stress, to prevent illness, and to enhance your appearance.

Health factors can have a big impact on what you do with your life and what career you pursue. You can't control certain health conditions, but you can do something about stress. Prolonged stress has a negative effect on your body. It can even affect your body's ability to prevent illness. Exercise your mind and body to relieve stress, to prevent illness, and to enhance your appearance.

Change, especially change in career direction, is often stressful. Changing jobs is one of the most stressful things you can do. Other highly stressful events are the death of a spouse, divorce, and financial problems. Stress-management experts have found that people who lose a job or face an uncertain future tend to experience more health problems and have more accidents than usual.

Total job satisfaction is rare because there are disadvantages to every job. Knowing what these disadvantages are and how to deal with them is an important part of planning your career and life's direction. If you are in a job that offers you no satisfaction, consider the following questions:

- Do the disadvantages of your current position outweigh the advantages?

- Is there something you can do to change the situation?

- Is it likely the situation will change if you do nothing and wait it out?

- Is your attitude toward the situation likely to change?

- Why did you accept the position? Is it part of your long-term career plan?

Often, a situation appears hopeless until you step back and reevaluate it objectively. If you can't be objective, talk with people whose opinions you value and trust. Many resources are available to help you identify and deal with work-related stress.

The following worksheet will show how vulnerable you are to stress. Evaluate yourself on each item. Refer to page 41 to score your responses.

How I Deal with Stress

1 = strongly disagree   **4** = slightly agree

2 = disagree   **5** = agree

3 = slightly disagree   **6** = strongly agree

I eat at least two balanced meals a day.	1	2	3	4	5	6
I get 7 to 8 hours of sleep each night.	1	2	3	4	5	6
I give and receive affection regularly.	1	2	3	4	5	6
I have several close relatives within 50 miles of my home on whom I can rely.	1	2	3	4	5	6
I exercise to the point of perspiration at least three times per week.	1	2	3	4	5	6
I seldom or never smoke.	1	2	3	4	5	6
I am the appropriate weight for my height.	1	2	3	4	5	6
I have an income adequate to meet basic expenses.	1	2	3	4	5	6
I get strength from my religious beliefs.	1	2	3	4	5	6
I regularly attend club or social activities.	1	2	3	4	5	6
I have fewer than three alcoholic drinks per week.	1	2	3	4	5	6
I have a strong network of friends and acquaintances.	1	2	3	4	5	6
I have several close friends I can confide in about personal matters.	1	2	3	4	5	6
I am in good health, including my eyes, ears, and teeth.	1	2	3	4	5	6
I am able to speak openly about my feelings when I'm angry or worried.	1	2	3	4	5	6
I have regular conversations with family members about problems, chores, money, and other daily-living issues.	1	2	3	4	5	6
I do something for fun at least once per week.	1	2	3	4	5	6
I am able to organize my time effectively.	1	2	3	4	5	6
I drink less than three cups of coffee, tea, and cola per day.	1	2	3	4	5	6
I take quiet time for myself during the day.	1	2	3	4	5	6

Total Stress Vulnerability Score = _____

Total Your Scores

If you have a score of **70 or more**, you generally have a low vulnerability to stress-related problems. However, looking for work can be more stressful than normal living. Take good care of yourself during your job search.

If you have a score from **41 through 69**, you are moderately vulnerable to stress-related problems. A stress-management plan will be important during your job search. Design a plan and stick with it.

If you have a score of **40 or less**, you are highly vulnerable to stress-related problems. Examine the items that received the lowest scores and make some changes in your life. A stress-management plan will be critical to your physical and emotional well being. Take this seriously.

Staying Physically Healthy

Dealing with stress and staying physically healthy are closely related. Taking care of your physical health helps relieve stress and enables you to manage life's changes successfully. Experts advise that two ways to stay healthy are to eat a balanced diet and exercise regularly.

Before starting any special diet or exercise program, consult with your doctor or with a certified professional nutritionist or trainer to determine the best course of action for your body's needs.

> Taking care of your physical health helps relieve stress and enables you to manage life's changes successfully. Before starting any special diet or exercise program, consult with your doctor or with a certified professional nutritionist or trainer to determine the best course of action for your body's needs.

People have various ways of coping with change, stress, and uncertain times. Some methods are more helpful than others. Eating well, exercising, and getting support are effective ways of coping with change. However, some people may add to their own problems. They may abuse alcohol or other substances, overeat, stop eating, stay in bed all day, or lose control of angry feelings and become violent. These are signals that a person isn't coping well. You can learn ways to cope differently. Agencies, people, or programs that can help are available in your community and are listed in your telephone book.

Eat a Balanced Diet

Machinery cannot operate without fuel, and your body cannot function well unless you provide it with a healthy, balanced diet. If you want help with eating well, the following people can provide guidance:

> Your body cannot function well unless you provide it with a healthy, balanced diet.

- Your doctor
- The nutrition expert at your local hospital or county health department
- Adult education programs or the cooperative extension service

Most of us already know the basic guidelines for healthy eating. You've also heard health warnings about the effects of too much or too little fat, fiber, salt, iron, vitamins, caffeine, and cholesterol. Many medical books and journals link poor health to a poor diet, and many cookbooks are devoted to special nutritional needs. Education and common sense should dictate which nutrients your body requires to keep you energized.

Exercise Regularly

Exercising uses up the excess adrenaline your body produces when under stress, and it produces helpful chemicals. These chemicals are called endorphins. They ease tension, improve mood, and create feelings of well-being. They serve as sort of a natural tranquilizer without the side effects of pills.

> Regular exercise helps your body's defenses ward off many illnesses, including those caused by stress.

Regular exercise helps your body's defenses ward off many illnesses, including those caused by stress. Keeping physically fit also helps you keep mentally fit. It's your best resource for keeping up with the rigorous demands of your everyday life. Before starting any exercise program, you should ask your doctor to help you determine the best type of activity for your body's needs.

The worksheet on page 40 titled "How I Deal with Stress" includes several responses that relate to keeping your physical body healthy. The following worksheet will help you think specifically about your strategy for staying physically healthy.

My Physical Health

I would describe my current physical health as _____

_____

_____

I have these concerns about my physical health: _____

_____

_____

One thing I could do to improve my eating habits is _____

_____

_____

One thing I could do to improve my exercise habits is _____

_____

_____

Finding Emotional Support

> ◆ **Tip** Difficult times in your life are easier to handle if you don't try to handle them alone.

As we have discussed, your ability to deal with stress is affected by your physical health. Your ability to deal with stress is also affected by your emotional health. Difficult times in your life are easier to handle if you don't try to handle them alone. You need an emotional support system. Various resources are available to provide job-seeking help, for example:

- Books or pamphlets that detail how to fill out job applications, write resumes or cover letters, and prepare for interviews

- Librarians or state employment service employees who can provide information about occupations and the local job market

- Friends or family who might offer to provide transportation, set up your resume, or care for your children while you go to an interview

- People in the community who have knowledge of possible job openings

Some people describe changing careers or looking for work as being on an emotional roller coaster. Feelings of relief, sadness, anger, depression, hope, disappointment, and excitement are all normal under these circumstances.

Regardless of the situation, most of us welcome the opportunity to talk about what we are going through. We feel better, think more clearly, and act more effectively. Unfortunately, those who are closest to us are often having difficulties of their own and may not be able to provide the support we need. For emotional support, talk to people who

- Have the ability to listen to your feelings

- Care about you but aren't emotionally involved in your situation

- Know how to give encouragement

- Have a positive attitude

- Believe in you and know what you can do

Generally, no one person is able to provide all the support you need. Think about your current support network and how you might expand it. Find a program for career planning. You will meet people who have had experiences similar to yours and people who are trained to give emotional support and encouragement.

The worksheet on page 40 titled "How I Deal with Stress" includes several responses that relate to finding emotional support. The following worksheet will help you think specifically about your strategy for maintaining your emotional health.

My Emotional Health

I would describe my current emotional health as _____

_____

_____

I have these concerns about my emotional health: _____

_____

_____

When I need to make a decision, I talk to _____

_____

_____

One way my emotional support system could be improved is _____

_____

_____

Life Roles

The term *life roles* refers to the way you function in a particular situation, what your part is in the overall picture. Your roles in life may include child, student, worker, parent, and partner. The roles you assume teach you various skills, provide you with opportunities, and help you set priorities.

Many factors work together to determine which roles you will assume in life. When you are deciding how to spend your time and energy, you think about what is important to you, your family, your background or culture, and your life. Ask yourself the following questions:

> The term *life roles* refers to the way you function in a particular situation, what your part is in the overall picture.

- Has my gender affected my role in life?

- Has my cultural or ethnic background determined what I am expected to do?

- What rules did my family have about who should do what?

- What current family circumstances affect the roles I now have?

- Do my past and current relationships affect my roles?

Life roles change. Sometimes you may be focused on only one role. At other times, you may be balancing several roles. As you plan your career, take into account the many roles you have had in the past, the roles you have now, and the roles you expect to have in the future.

The following worksheet will help you think about how your roles change. The first part of the worksheet is a list of roles you may now have. Not all of the roles will apply to you, so just skip the ones that do not. Briefly describe each of your current roles. In the last part of the worksheet, list your past roles and probable future roles. The first part of the worksheet can give you some possibilities.

My Changing Life Roles

The check marks below indicate life roles I currently have. I've briefly described each of these roles.

_____ Student_____

_____ Spouse or partner _____

_____ Homemaker _____

_____ Parent _____

_____ Person of leisure _____

_____ Citizen _____

_____ Child _____

_____ Employer _____

_____ Employee_____

_____ Job seeker _____

_____ Other _____

Roles I've had in the past: _____

_____

_____

_____

Roles I expect to have in the future: _____

_____

_____

_____

As you consider your current life roles, think about how you will balance these roles. If you are thinking of returning to school or work or changing your career direction, you will have to make room in your life for a new role. Think about how much time and energy each of your current roles takes. Think about which of your life roles has the greatest priority.

If you find you need assistance in sorting out your thoughts about your roles, talk with a close friend or consult a professional.

You have looked at your past, current, and future roles and how your roles balance. Complete the following worksheet and consider how your life roles affect your career decisions.

My Life Roles and Career Decisions

Roles that give me experiences and help me develop the skills I need to make career changes:

_____

_____

Roles that play a part in helping me reach my career goals:

_____

_____

_____

Roles that hinder my career planning:

_____

_____

_____

Changes I would like to make in the roles I now have:

_____

_____

I am satisfied with the following aspects of my current balance of roles:

_____

_____

Current roles that may affect my goals and dreams for the future:

_____

_____

Roles I may have assumed without thinking about how they affect my future goals:

_____

_____

Roles I assumed because someone else expected me to do so:

_____

_____

Career Interests

Another element of career satisfaction is to find an occupation of interest to you. You will want to think about specific jobs. Your local librarian can help you find books that provide lists of jobs. We recommend you look at the list of jobs compiled by the U.S. Department of Labor (DOL). This list appears in the *Occupational Outlook Handbook*, which can be purchased through JIST Works or through the DOL. The jobs are also listed at www.bls.gov/oco.

After you have looked at a list of jobs, complete the following worksheet. In the left column, list jobs you could do with the skills and abilities you have now. In the right column, list jobs that interest you but that would require additional training, education, or experience. Even if you don't have the necessary job qualifications now, don't discard an occupational area in which you are truly interested.

Jobs That Interest Me

Jobs I could get with the skills and knowledge I have now

Jobs that interest me but that would require additional training, education, or experience

JIST Works publishes a book titled *Guide for Occupational Exploration (GOE)*, Third Edition. This book is based on information from the U.S. Department of Labor and organizes jobs into 14 interest areas. For each job, the *GOE* provides the information such as job duties, required level of training and education, personality type needed, average salary, projected growth, skills required, and physical and work conditions.

> Keep your interests in mind as you look at career possibilities.

Read the descriptions of the 14 interest areas on the following worksheet. Check any that interest you. Then select and number the three areas that you find most interesting. Put *1* next to the area that interests you most, *2* by the next most interesting, and *3* by your third choice. Keep your interests in mind as you look at career possibilities. You also should consider areas that might interest you if you learned more about them.

My Career Interests

My main interests are in the following areas:

_____ **Arts, Entertainment, and Media.** I have an interest in creatively expressing my feelings and ideas, in communicating news and information, or in performing.

_____ **Science, Math, and Engineering.** I have an interest in discovering and analyzing information about the natural world. I have an interest in applying scientific research to problems in medicine, the life sciences, and the natural sciences. I have an interest in imagining and manipulating quantitative data. I have an interest in applying technology to manufacturing, transportation, mining, and other economic activities.

_____ **Plants and Animals.** I have an interest in working with plants and animals, usually outdoors.

_____ **Law, Law Enforcement, and Public Safety.** I have an interest in upholding people's rights or in protecting people and property by using authority, inspecting, or monitoring.

_____ **Mechanics, Installers, and Repairers.** I have an interest in applying mechanical, electrical, or electronic principles to practical situations by use of machines or hand tools.

_____ **Construction, Mining, and Drilling.** I have an interest in assembling components of buildings and other structures, or in using mechanical devices to drill or excavate.

_____ **Transportation.** I have an interest in operations that move people or materials.

_____ **Industrial Production.** I have an interest in repetitive, concrete, organized activities most often done in a factory setting.

_____ **Business Detail.** I have an interest in organized, clearly defined activities that require accuracy and attention to detail, primarily in an office setting.

_____ **Sales and Marketing.** I have an interest in bringing others to a particular point of view by personal persuasion, using sales and promotional techniques.

_____ **Recreation, Travel, and Other Services.** I have an interest in catering to the personal wishes and needs of others, so that they can enjoy cleanliness, good food and drinks, comfortable lodging away from home, and enjoyable recreation.

_____ **Education and Social Service.** I have an interest in teaching people or improving their social or spiritual well-being.

_____ **General Management and Support.** I have an interest in making an organization run smoothly.

_____ **Medical and Health Services.** I have an interest in helping people be healthy.

▶*LET'S REVIEW*

Place a check mark beside each statement that describes you. Review information in this chapter that applies to any statements you are unable to check.

Self-Assessment Checklist

_____ I can describe what I value in my life and in my career.

_____ I know what my preferred style of learning is.

_____ I can describe my personality traits.

_____ I know how to make decisions.

_____ I know what my risk-taking style is, and I know how it affects the decisions I make.

_____ I am able to manage my time effectively.

_____ I know some steps to take in dealing with stress.

_____ I understand how eating well and exercising impact my physical health.

_____ I have a support system that helps me maintain my emotional health.

_____ I can identify my past, current, and future life roles, and I know how these affect my career planning.

_____ I know what type of work interests me most.

Date: _____

Chapter 4

What You Have to Offer

In Chapter 3, you focused on understanding who you are. You considered what to include in your portfolio to document your values and your personal goals and history. The next step is to think about what you have to offer a prospective employer. This chapter will help you answer these questions:

- What work experience do I have that would be of interest to an employer?

- What experience have I acquired in nonwork activities?

- What have I accomplished in my life and work?

- What skills have I developed?

- What education and training have I received?

- What have other people said about my knowledge, skills, performance, and accomplishments?

If you choose, you can include the worksheets in this chapter in your portfolio. You may want to put them in one of these sections: Accomplishments and Job History, Skills and Attributes, Education and Training, or Testimonials and Recommendations. Of course, you can decide where the worksheets fit best in your portfolio, based on how you decide to organize your documents. The worksheets are for your reference only. They are not designed to be shown to employers.

Job History

As you build your portfolio, you may think that the only work to take into account is your paid employment. If so, you underestimate what you have to offer. You have developed skills and built experiences from every part of your life, whether work related and nonwork related.

> You have developed skills and built experiences from every part of your life.

Paid Employment

Before completing the following worksheet, you may want to make several copies of it so you can have information about all of your jobs. (You have the publisher's permission to make as many copies of this worksheet as you need.) If you don't have access to a copy machine, you can use the worksheet as a guide and write your job information on separate sheets of paper.

For each of your current and past jobs, complete a worksheet with information about your employer and your job. List responsibilities you had in each. Write as much about your job duties as possible. This will help you decide which tasks were your most important.

> Employers prefer to talk to people who know what you can do and who have worked with you. Employers do not think references from friends and family are reliable. Be sure to ask people in advance if they will serve as a reference.

Also, for each job, think of someone who could serve as a reference for you. Remember that employers prefer to talk to people who know what you can do and who have worked with you. Coworkers, former employers, and others who have firsthand knowledge of your skills and strengths can be valuable references. Employers do not think references from friends and family are reliable. Be sure to ask people in advance if they will serve as a reference. Contacting these people in advance ensures that they won't be caught off-guard when an employer calls. Remember it's up to you to educate your references regarding the kind of information you want them to share with employers.

Include the completed worksheets in your portfolio. You can then refer to them when you are filling out job applications or talking to an employer.

My Paid Employment

Job title: _____

Name of employer/organization/contact person:_____

_____

Employer's phone:_____Employer's fax: _____

Employer's street address: _____

City/State/ZIP:_____

Dates: _____

Tasks performed: _____

_____

_____

_____

Person who could provide a reference for me related to this job: _____

_____

Person's address: _____

_____

Person's phone/fax: _____

Person's e-mail: _____

Job title: _____

Name of employer/organization/contact person:_____

_____

Employer's phone:_____Employer's fax: _____

Employer's street address: _____

City/State/ZIP:_____

Dates: _____

Tasks performed: _____

_____

_____

_____

Person who could provide a reference for me related to this job: _____

_____

Person's address: _____

_____

Person's phone/fax: _____

Person's e-mail: _____

Nonwork Experience

Activities you do in your nonwork time are important clues in deciding on an occupation. The activities you choose to do around your home, for your community, and for other people in your leisure time are things you want to do.

> Activities you do in your nonwork time are important clues in deciding on an occupation.

These activities can help you develop skills you can use on the job. In your portfolio, include examples, photographs, programs, or other materials that show what you've learned or accomplished by participating in these nonwork activities.

On the following worksheet, list your nonwork activities such as serving on a committee at your child's school, teaching a class at your church, participating in political functions, working with a youth sport team, or organizing community projects for your social club. Complete the statements, and then put a check mark beside the activities you could do for pay.

My Nonwork Experience

I have been involved in many activities not related to work. I've listed some of them below. I've also placed a check mark beside the activities I think I could also do in a job.

At home, I do the following jobs:

_____

_____

_____

_____

In my spare time, I do these activities:

_____

_____

_____

_____

In my community, I am active in:

_____

_____

_____

_____

Accomplishments

Tip You gain greater satisfaction from doing work that lets you use your skills. Focus on what you have done that makes you proud.

Throughout your life, you have done things that gave you a great sense of accomplishment. Perhaps you did something like that many years ago, or maybe just yesterday. Perhaps you did something big, or maybe something small. You may or may not have received personal recognition, but what you did mattered to you.

Looking at these accomplishments can help you identify your skills. The skills you used in your great accomplishments are your most powerful skills. Chances are, you are good at and enjoy using these skills. If you can identify these skills and use them in your current and future jobs, you have a better chance at succeeding in your career. Also, you probably will gain greater satisfaction from doing work that lets you use your skills.

As you consider your career plans, avoid focusing on any failures you've experienced. Instead, focus on what you have done that makes you proud. This will strengthen your self-confidence and help you identify skills and abilities that will interest future employers.

Don't underestimate the importance of what you have accomplished. In all of your experiences, look for the skills you have developed. For example:

- If you have helped your friends do something, you may have learned to work as part of a team and you may have developed problem-solving skills.

- If you have raised a family, you have probably developed people skills and a sense of responsibility and dependability.

- If you run a household you may know how to budget your money, stay organized, and manage your time.

- If you have taken steps to keep physically fit and healthy, you probably have high energy, discipline, and motivation.

As you complete the following worksheet, list your accomplishments and other activities that you are proud of. Consider all your life experiences.

My Accomplishments

Three things I've done at work that I am really proud of are

1. _____
   _____

2. _____
   _____

3. _____
   _____

Three things I've done in nonwork activities that I'm really proud of are

1. _____
   _____

2. _____
   _____

3. _____
   _____

Skills and Attributes

One of the most important things you can do before deciding on or changing your career is to identify all your skills. You can then emphasize your most valuable skills and communicate to employers not only what you have done but how well you did it.

> Remember that there is a difference between what you do and what you *can* do. The skills you have make you a unique individual.

Often people who are in the middle of a job or career decision think of their abilities in terms of their job titles. People getting their first jobs worry that employers won't think they have skills because they have no previous work experience. The truth is that many skills are transferable from job to job. Also, skills that are developed in school, in the home, and in volunteer situations are often transferable to job situations. And, many skills that are important to employers are those that relate to your personality and that make you a good worker.

In the book *The Quick Job Search: Seven Steps to Getting a Good Job in Less Time,* published by JIST Works, author Michael Farr identifies three types of skills:

- **Self-Management Skills.** These are skills that spring from your basic personality and your ability to adapt to new situations. These skills are an indication of the kind of worker you will be. Flexibility, friendliness, and punctuality are examples of self-management skills.

- **Transferable Skills.** These are skills that can be used in various jobs. They may be learned in one job, but they can also be used in other jobs. Meeting deadlines, supervising people, and writing clearly are examples of transferable skills.

- **Job-Related Skills.** These are skills you must have to be able to do a particular job. While these specific skills would not be required in most jobs, they would be essential in certain jobs. Being able to drive a truck, prepare a teaching plan, or interpret a heart monitor are examples of job-related skills.

If you need additional help in identifying and documenting your skills, many books and other materials are available at your local library or bookstore. Talk with friends and coworkers. Ask them what they think are your most important skills. Remember that a skill is simply something you can do well. You probably have hundreds of skills, not just a few.

Also, remember that there is a difference between what you do and what you *can* do. The skills you have make you a unique individual. Your skills will change over time, and some skills will continue to develop more than others. You are likely to change jobs and careers more than once in your lifetime. Your ability to transfer your skills and adapt to a new career is very important. People who understand and communicate their skills well make job and career changes more easily than people who do not.

The following table illustrates how you might document skills in your portfolio.

Skill	How I Demonstrate This Skill	What I Can Include in My Portfolio
Self-management	I'm always on time for work.	My annual review
Negotiation	I wrote a chores contract for my family.	Copy of the family contract
Organization	I planned and organized all the activities for my high school reunion.	Letters to other committee members, copy of reunion program listing my name
Diplomatic	I helped my company reduce customer complaints by more than 30 percent.	Copy of my proposal plan, letter of commendation from my supervisor
Hardworking	I was Employee of the Month at my new company after only six months on the job.	Employee of the Month certificate

If you have trouble thinking of what to include in your portfolio, talk to a friend, family member, or coworker who can help you.

Refer to this table as you complete the following worksheet. Place check marks beside the skills you have. Think how you have demonstrated those skills. Then think about what you can include in your portfolio that would document that skill. Include in your portfolio the documentation that shows that you have these skills.

My Skills—Demonstrated and Documented

Skill	How I Demonstrate This Skill	What I Can Include in My Portfolio
_____ Communication	_____	_____
_____ Computer literacy	_____	_____
_____ Decision making	_____	_____
_____ Dependability	_____	_____
_____ Flexibility	_____	_____
_____ Initiative	_____	_____
_____ Integrity/honesty	_____	_____
_____ Creativity	_____	_____
_____ Cooperation	_____	_____
_____ Critical thinking	_____	_____
_____ Leadership	_____	_____
_____ Analysis	_____	_____
_____ Budget management	_____	_____
_____ Listening	_____	_____
_____ Persistence	_____	_____
_____ Problem solving	_____	_____
_____ Reading	_____	_____
_____ Responsibility	_____	_____
_____ Mathematics	_____	_____
_____ Teamwork	_____	_____
_____ Speaking	_____	_____
_____ Negotiation	_____	_____
_____ Self-esteem	_____	_____
_____ Self-management	_____	_____
_____ Tolerance	_____	_____
_____ Other	_____	_____

Education and Training

In the Education and Training section of your portfolio, you may want to include the following documents and information:

- Apprenticeships
- Certificates
- Continuing Education Units (CEUs)
- Courses completed
- Diplomas
- Favorite school subjects
- General Educational Development certificate (GED)
- Internships
- Languages
- Licenses
- Military training
- On-the-job training
- Things you have taught yourself
- Transcripts
- Volunteer service
- Workshops

> This section can include any material or stories from your life that show what you've learned in school or from someone else.

Documentation also could include any material or stories from your life that show what you've learned in school or from someone else. It might include what you have done on the job or in your home or community. It might be something you did just for yourself. Your portfolio is a good place to store this material.

Testimonials and Recommendations

 Most people do not want to brag about what they've done. However, remember that it's okay to share the good feedback you receive from other people.

As you review your work experiences, remember to include in your portfolio any commendations, awards, letters of recognition, performance evaluations, and positive comments by supervisors, coworkers, customers, or clients.

You may hesitate to include testimonials and recommendations in your portfolio. Most people do not want to brag about what they've done. However, remember that it's okay to share the good feedback you receive from other people. Keep any documents you have that indicate you have done something that made a difference in someone's work or life.

Life Changes

One sure fact of life is that things constantly change. You have undoubtedly experienced and managed many changes in your life. These changes might include

- Going to school for the first time

- Moving

- Leaving home

- Taking your first job

- Changing jobs

- Having children

- Entering into a new relationship

- Leaving a relationship

> If you want to improve your work or situation, you will have to make some changes.

Many people do not like change. It means letting go of the familiar and moving toward the unknown. However, it is possible to think of change as a challenge. If you want to improve your work or situation, you will have to make some changes.

Overcoming Fear

No matter what type of change you are contemplating—change in your career, schooling, location, or personal status—fear often accompanies change. In her book *Dare to Change Your Job and Your Life*, published by JIST Works, author Carole Kanchier says this about fear:

> Fear often accompanies change. By identifying your fears, you can deal with them openly and honestly.

> *"Fears can be barriers to your progress. Growing, which is really just a matter of abandoning a comfortable position, usually involves pain. Trying to avoid pain by constructing rigid roles, defenses, viewpoints, or excuses only makes the process more difficult. The first and most important risk you can take is to be honest with yourself. Acknowledge your fears. Like all emotions, fear has a purpose; it alerts you to take action to protect yourself from loss."*

By identifying your fears, you can deal with them openly and honestly. All of us can learn to face change without fear. Taking action to overcome your barriers is the first step. Use the following worksheet to help you think about the changes in your life and how you handle such changes.

I Make Changes

Two things I fear or dislike about change are

1. _____

_____

2. _____

_____

Two things that excite me about change are

1. _____

_____

2. _____

_____

Two things I have learned about myself from the changes I've faced are

1. _____

_____

2. _____

_____

Overcoming Life's Barriers

When we succeed at something, it gives us more confidence to try again. You have accomplished many things on the job and in nonwork activities. As an adult, you also recognize that setbacks can and do occur. However, these setbacks can usually be overcome and can even be good learning experiences.

> Life doesn't stand still, it changes. You can choose to stand still and be left behind, or you can choose to grow and pursue new opportunities.

Life doesn't stand still, it changes. The economy changes. Industries and employment opportunities change. Jobs come and go. You can choose to stand still and be left behind, or you can choose to grow and pursue new opportunities.

You may have circumstances in your life that hold you back from making the changes you want to make. They are barriers that hinder you or prevent you from reaching a goal, fulfilling a dream, or making a change. Creating your portfolio helps you examine all the possibilities open to you. And it makes you aware of barriers you may be facing.

You may feel that you are not free to make all the choices you would like to make. You may feel that responsibilities, money, or other realities limit your options. Sometimes these circumstances are ones you can't change. If so, you have to make other choices. Often, however, you may be overlooking the possibilities. You may be able to overcome a barrier if you think creatively.

If your feel that there is a barrier in your life that keeps you from making the changes you want or from reaching your goals, ask yourself the following questions:

- Is the barrier something I have built for myself, or is the situation really beyond my control?
- Can I change my way of thinking about the barrier?
- Are there ways around this barrier that I haven't considered?

On the following worksheet, place a check mark beside each item that is or could be a barrier for you. Briefly describe what you could do to overcome that barrier. For example, you may want to change jobs but don't have the educational background required for the job you want. To remove the barrier, you might have to sign up for evening classes and spread your education out over several years. Even if it takes time, you will eventually be able to improve your life and get the job you want.

My Personal Barriers

The items I've checked below are my personal barriers. I've described what I might be able to do to overcome each barrier I've checked.

_____ Transportation _____

_____

_____

_____ Budget _____

_____

_____

_____ Education _____

_____

_____

_____ Appearance/Clothing _____

_____

_____

_____ Family responsibilities _____

_____

_____

_____ Gender _____

_____

_____

_____ Other _____

_____

_____

_____

You now have a list of ideas about what can you do to remove the barriers in your life. Ask other people to help you expand your list. Include ideas that sound silly or impossible. Sometimes a silly-sounding idea may lead you to a solution. When you think your list is complete, pick one or two ideas and try them.

If you think your barriers are too great for you to overcome by yourself, seek out professional counselors who can help you. If you have trouble changing or accepting your limitations, many publications are available to help you work through these issues. Don't expect to change your life all at once. Trying to make too many changes at one time can be overwhelming.

▶ *LET'S REVIEW*

Place a check mark beside each statement that describes you. Review information in this chapter that applies to any statements you are unable to check.

Self-Assessment Checklist

_____ I have gathered information about my work experience.

_____ I can identify experience I have gained through my home, leisure, and community activities.

_____ I can identify my achievements related to work, learning, and leisure.

_____ I can explain the different types of skills.

_____ I have thought about the skills I have and how I demonstrated those skills in the past.

_____ I know what items to include in my portfolio to document my skills.

_____ I have several ideas about what to include in the Education and Training section of my portfolio.

_____ I have several ideas about what to include in the Testimonials and Recommendations section of my portfolio.

_____ I can describe ways to cope during change and transition.

_____ I can name changes I've gone through.

Date: _____

Part Three

Reaching Your Career Goals

Chapter 5

Exploring Career Options

In previous chapters of this book, you have learned to organize and use your portfolio. You have also increased your understanding of who you are and what you have to offer. This chapter will help you answer the following questions:

- How can I keep track of information about careers I've researched?

- What kind of job do I envision as being perfect for me?

- What are some sources I can rely on for general career information?

- What are some sources I can turn to for information about specific careers?

- What options are available to me for getting additional training or education?

- Do I have what it takes to be self-employed?

Consider including the worksheets and checklists in this chapter in your portfolio. These are not items you would want to show to an employer, but they will serve as valuable references as you look for a job.

Gathering Career Information

Whether you are looking for your first job, trying to move up in a company, or making a career change, you need to explore occupations and the labor market. The world of work changes rapidly, so you must understand the changes in jobs.

Exploring careers gives you a chance to consider the positive and negative aspects of various occupations. You can then weigh these against your own values and what is most important to you.

When you are exploring careers, you will gather information about specific jobs and occupations. For example:

> Exploring careers gives you a chance to consider the positive and negative aspects of various occupations.

- The nature of the work

- The industries that include these occupations

- Training or education required

- Working conditions

- Employment trends and advancement possibilities

- Related occupations

- How well your values, interests, education, skills, and abilities match

Keep track of all the details you find out about an occupation. There are many sources of good career information. Research the labor market to learn about

- National, state, and local employment trends

- Occupations and industries that are growing, staying the same, or declining

- Current or anticipated job openings

Refer to several sources of information and look into a number of possibilities. Use the following worksheet to track all your career research about a certain occupation. You may not be able to complete the worksheet now, but you should be able to complete it as you work through this chapter and follow up on its suggestions.

Before writing, make a photocopy for each occupation that interests you. Look at the work you did in Chapter 3 to find job titles that interest you.

My Career Research

Name of occupation: _____

Source of information: _____

Tasks, responsibilities, risks, and physical demands of this occupation:

_____
_____
_____

Skills required to do this job:	I have this skill.
_____	_____
_____	_____
_____	_____
_____	_____

Workload in this job: _____

Pace of work in this job: _____

Looks, sounds, and smells associated with this job:

_____
_____
_____

People in this job work _____ hours per day.

People in this job work _____ days per week.

People in this job work _____ hours of overtime per week.

People in this job travel _____ days per year.

Training, education, or other qualifications (licenses, registration, certification) required for this job:

_____
_____
_____
_____

Salary range for this job: _____

_____
_____

Employment outlook for the future of this occupation:

_____

_____

Possibilities for advancement or promotion:

_____

_____

_____

_____

Related occupations:

_____

_____

_____

Sources of additional information (books, schools, people, Web sites):

_____

_____

_____

_____

The Perfect Job for You

Before you begin looking at career options, think about what your ideal job would be like. Think about the job that you've always wanted or that would meet most of your needs. Also consider what you know about yourself.

Few people work in an occupation that is ideal in every way. But the more you focus on what you want, the closer you will get to finding your ideal job. As you complete the following worksheet, imagine yourself in your perfect or ideal job.

> The more you focus on what you want, the closer you will get to finding your ideal job.

My Perfect Job

In my perfect job, I would stay in the United States. yes _____ no _____

The region of the country I would work in is _____

_____

The climate where my ideal job is would be_____

The size of city I would work in is _____

I would work in   _____ an urban setting   _____ a rural setting

In my ideal job I would work   _____ inside   _____ outside

I would work for

_____ a big company   _____ a midsize company   _____ a small company

I would   _____ stay in one place   _____ move around

In my ideal job I would want to wear clothes that are _____

_____

My ideal work site would have some kind of equipment in it.   _____ yes   _____ no

Tasks and Responsibilities

My ideal job would involve   _____ physical tasks   _____ mental tasks

The amount of time I would spend working with data and information: _____

The amount of time I would spend working with people: _____

The number of people I would work with: _____

The amount of time I would spend working with equipment: _____

I would be   _____ a leader   _____ a follower

I would be   _____ a planner   _____ a doer

The skills I would use in my ideal job:_____

_____

During a typical work day, I would _____

_____

In my ideal job, I would have a boss who is _____

I would be the boss or supervisor. _____ yes   _____ no

I would be part of a team. _____ yes   _____ no

The number of people working with me would be _____

My coworkers in my ideal job could be described as _____

I would work alone. _____ yes   _____ no

Sources of Career Information

As you research career options, you may feel over-loaded with information about jobs, industries, and opportunities. Knowing what you consider to be the perfect job helps you discover what you want in your next job. Newspapers, magazines, television, radio, the Web, and friends all provide tidbits of information about career opportunities and jobs. But before relying on career-related information, ask yourself these questions:

> Do not disregard a major career interest because you uncover some negative information. Continue exploring all your interests.

- **Is the information up to date?** A five-year-old survey is not as reliable as one completed in the past year. Career information rapidly becomes obsolete. Sometimes there is a time lag between gathering and publishing survey results.

- **Is the information accurate?** Information passes through many sources and may be slanted or misinterpreted. Always consider the source of the information.

- **Is the information unbiased?** Think about whether the source has a reason to select only parts of the information or to slant the conclusions. For example: Someone recruiting you to take a training program or class may not be objective about the value of the training. Or if you talk with someone who is not happy in his or her job, you may get information that has a negative slant.

- **Is the information confirmed by other sources?** Another way to judge information involves seeing, hearing, and reading the information in many sources. For example, if five people give you the same information about a career, you can probably rely on that information. If government data and a career counselor confirm what you've heard, your confidence in the information increases.

Do not disregard a major career interest because you uncover some negative information. Continue exploring until you are satisfied you have all the information you need. Then you can make an informed and responsible decision. Remember, trust your own judgment above all else. The following information describes tools you can use to explore your career options.

Informational Interviews

The purpose of an informational interview is to gain information, *not* to interview for a job opening. Request an informational interview with someone who works in a career area that interests you.

The following list gives examples of informational interview questions. Design and add your own questions to ensure you walk away from the interview with the information you need. Be sensitive to not asking questions the person you interview might find too personal. For example, specific questions about salary are not usually appropriate.

> The purpose of an informational interview is to gain information, not to interview for a job opening.

My Informational Interviews

General Questions to Ask

Preparation

- What credentials or degrees are required for entry into this kind of work?

- What types of prior experience are absolutely essential?

- How did you prepare for this kind of work?

Present Job

- What do you do during a typical work week?

- What are the major tasks of your job?

- What skills or talents are most essential for effective performance in this job?

- How would you describe your work environment?

- What is the general pay range for this type work?

- What are the toughest problems you deal with on a day-to-day basis?

- What do you find most rewarding about this job?

- If you were to leave this kind of work, what factors might contribute to your decision?

Life Style

- What obligations does your work put on your personal time?

- How much flexibility do you have in terms of dress, hours of work, vacation schedule, and place of residence?

- How often do people in your line of work change jobs?

Career Future and Alternatives

- If things develop as you would like, what career goals would you like to achieve?

- How rapidly is your present career field growing?

- How would you describe or estimate future prospects?

- If the work you do was suddenly eliminated, what other type of work do you feel you could do?

- What companies hire people with your background?

Job Hunting

- How do people find out about jobs in your career area? Are they advertised in the newspaper or professional journals? If so, which ones? Is the information sent out by word of mouth? If so, who spreads the word? Is the information sent out by your personnel department?

- How does a person move from one position to another in this type work?

- If you were to hire someone to work with you today, which of the following factors would be the most important in your hiring decision? Why?

    Educational credentials

    Personality, personal attributes

    Past work experience

    Applicant's knowledge of the organization and job

    Specific skills and talents

    Other

Advice

- How well suited is my background for this type of work?

- Can you suggest other related fields?

- What types of paid employment or other experience would you most strongly recommend?

- If you were just entering the workforce, what would you do differently to prepare for this occupation? What coursework would you take? What kinds of practical experience would you try to get?

Referral to Others

- Based on our conversation today, can you suggest other people who may be able to provide me with additional information?

- Can you suggest a few people who might be willing to see me?

- May I use your name when I contact the people you suggest?

Job-Specific Questions to Ask

If you determine during the interview that you might be interested in working for the organization where the person you are interviewing works, consider asking the following questions.

- What does your organization do?

- What is the size of your organization?

- What are the geographical locations of your organization?

- What is the average length of time employees stay with the organization?

- How much freedom is given to new people?

- What types of formal or on-the-job training does the organization provide?

- How often are performance reviews given?

- What are the procedures for transferring from one division to another?

- How much decision-making authority is given to an employee after one year?

- What new product lines or services is the company developing?

- Is the organization expanding? If so, where?

- How does the organization compare to its competition?

Job Shadowing

When you job shadow, you go to work with someone for a day, a few days, or even a week to observe all aspects of the person's occupation. This is an excellent method for seeing firsthand what a person in a job really does.

> Job shadowing allows you to see firsthand what a person in a job really does.

Job Clubs

You can find these programs in community organizations, government agencies, outplacement firms, or schools. Job clubs train job seekers in how to look for work and how to locate and contact employers. A job club also provides practical help such as a base for job hunting, employer listings, and office equipment. Program leaders and other job seekers provide structure, emotional support, and encouragement.

Career Information Systems

Computerized information systems may be available within your local community. Contact your library, nearby high school or college, or state employment office for this service. Many systems match information about you to possible occupations. Some systems provide job information such as work descriptions, skills required, training or education required, pay ranges, and related jobs.

Career Resource Centers

Career resource centers provide many sources of information in one place. They may be located in large businesses, schools, colleges and universities, libraries, or government or community agencies. Information may be in the form of books, journal articles, microfiche, video- and audiotapes, CD-ROMs, and computer diskettes.

Outplacement Centers

These services often share information about job openings and employer lists. They may also provide resume-writing assistance, interview training, or career coaching.

The Internet

Start with government sites such as http://online.onetcenter.org. Another option is www.jist.com.

Networking

Tip To network effectively, you must tell people what you do, what you do well, and what you want to do.

Exploring career possibilities is simply a matter of making connections (*networking*) with people and information. Statistically, networking is the best way to find a job. And it's not difficult to do. You already know many people. The people you know also know many people. These people are all part of your network.

The purpose of networking is to get information that can lead you to a job. Look for someone who will sponsor you. Get permission to use that person's name to introduce yourself to new job opportunities. Send a thank-you note for any information you receive from the people in your network. To network effectively, you must tell people what you do, what you do well, and what you want to do.

Your network can help you find out about various occupations and develop leads on interesting career options. Start with your family; then go to your friends, former employers, or coworkers for help. Also, talk with people you've met while volunteering in community activities or school organizations. They may know someone who could help you explore other career areas.

Many people you ask will tell you they don't know anyone who could help you. They're probably thinking only in terms of someone who could actually give you a job. You have to be persistent and help the people in your network understand what you are after. A person may not be able to give you the name of someone who can help you directly, but he or she may give you the name of someone who can give you the name of someone else. And that person may be able to help you.

When you network, start from a broad perspective. Memorize the following five "I" words to help you remember what you need to do:

- **Identify** what you want to do and what you do well. Determine what industry needs you.

- **Investigate** available networking resources.

- **Initiate** a strategy. Use your resume as a brochure. Talk to people. Research and explore.

- **Imitate** people who are successful. Find out what works for them and how they got where they are. Follow in their footsteps.

- **Incorporate** and use all the information and resources you gather. Keep your perspective broad.

Expand your network by adding names and phone numbers of people you meet while exploring careers. When you talk with someone about career options, ask them if they can recommend others who might help you. Ask each person you know to give you the names and phone numbers of three people who might be able to help you. Contact those people and ask them for the names and numbers of three more people. Very quickly you will have a large network that can help you find the information you want.

When you network, collect business cards, flyers, and brochures from people and businesses that interest you. Store these materials in your portfolio.

After you decide on your new career direction, get back in touch with your network. Then use your network to help you find a position. After you are hired, make sure you let the people in your network know about your situation and thank them for their assistance.

The following diagram illustrates a structured way of thinking about a network.

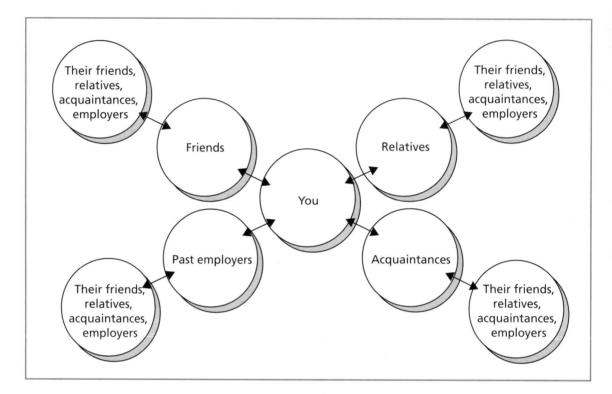

Use the following worksheet to record information about your own network. Add more pages as you need them. Use actual names of people wherever possible. Remember, these people can help you discover career options now and find a job later.

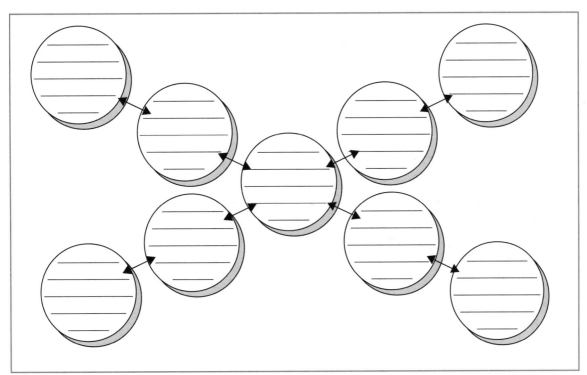

Training Options

Consider now how you will get the education, training, and experience for the careers that interest you. Generally, the more education or training you have, the more pay you receive. So it may be well worth the extra time and money to qualify yourself for a job that interests you.

> **Tip** Consider now how you will get the education, training, and experience for the careers that interest you.

As you explore various occupations, don't exclude those that require more training or education than you have now. Average earnings for college graduates are considerably higher than for those without college degrees. Consider the earnings impact of higher education as you look at jobs. Here are some sources of information about education and training options:

- Adult education program
- Apprenticeship council

- Armed forces processing center
- High school guidance office
- Human resources department
- Job training office
- Local college or university
- State employment office
- Technical college
- Veteran's services center
- Women's center

As you can see, there are many training options available. Some are short classes and others may take a year or two. As you gather information about education or training options, keep the following ideas in mind:

- **Get the employer's viewpoint.** Employers sometimes recruit from certain training programs and not others. If you are considering more education or training for a particular career, talk with employers before you enroll. Ask them what they think of the program you are considering. Ask if they prefer to hire from a specific program.

- **Comparison shop.** Just as tuition and fees vary from one school to another, so does training. Call a number of programs to compare the quality and cost. Consider the time of day classes are held and the length of the program. Ask if you can get credit for work experience and whether you can take courses by correspondence or other alternative means.

- **Find out about accreditation.** Most schools (public or private, college or university, trade or technical), are certified by a national organization. This organization determines if the program offers good-quality training. Ask if the school is accredited, and if so, by what organization. If you are in doubt, your state department of education will know the answer or can refer you to someone who does.

- **Ask about financial aid or tuition assistance.** Don't rule out more training or education because of your financial situation. Most schools have financial aid programs. Special programs in your area may provide funds for training. Find out if you qualify. If you are currently working, your place of employment may help you get training or further education by paying all or part of the costs.

In the future, more jobs will require some education or technical training beyond high school. As a result, many adults are returning to school or specialized training. In fact, many people with four-year college degrees are now returning to school to receive a two-year degree in a technical field. You may want to invest in more education to find a career that interests you.

The following worksheet lists ways to upgrade your knowledge and training. Check those you are interested in pursuing. Use your network, the library, or high school or community college counseling offices to find out what training programs are offered in your area.

I Explore Training Options

I could get more training by...	Where	When
❏ Reading journals or books		
❏ Attending workshops		
❏ Beginning an apprenticeship program		
❏ Beginning a job-training program		
❏ Enrolling in a trade, technical, or vocational school		
❏ Enrolling in a degree program		
❏ Two-year program		
❏ Four-year program		
❏ Masters program		
❏ Other degree program		
❏ Enrolling in informal courses		
❏ Enrolling in company-sponsored courses		
❏ Getting a license or certificate		
❏ Joining the military		
❏ Taking a temporary job that would add to my skills		
❏ Other		

Self-Employment

Small-business startups comprise one of the fastest growing segments of our economy. One growing trend involves large companies contracting with small businesses to provide services. As these companies hire more short-term, temporary, or contract help, many people find themselves working for a number of employers. Without even planning for it, they have become small businesses.

> One of the best things about self-employment is that **you** define what *success* means.

One of the best things about self-employment is that **you** define what *success* means, based largely on your reasons for wanting to start your own business. No matter what your reasons, most people find there is a certain satisfaction in turning their self-employment dream into something real.

Owning and running your own business calls for different skills than working for someone else. You can acquire the necessary skills and knowledge by attending classes on how to set up a small business. Some of what it takes to succeed in a small business depends on your abilities, personal management skills, and available resources.

If you want to pursue self-employment, research all options carefully. Various assessments are available to introduce you to the many characteristics of successful entrepreneurs. You can use these forms to assess your own entrepreneurial characteristics. Three main ways to become self-employed are

- To start a new business based on your own idea

- To purchase an existing business from someone else

- To buy a franchise

Before starting your own business, you might want to work for someone else who is in your chosen field. By doing so, you can acquire the skills and experiences you will need. No matter what you decide, remember to research all options.

To begin your own business you must

- Decide on the legal status of your business (sole proprietorship, partnership, limited partnership, or corporation)

- Write your business plan

- Finance your operation

> Talk to other small-business owners about their experiences, joys, problems, mistakes, and successes.

Many resources are available to help individuals become self-employed: chambers of commerce, economic development agencies, small-business development centers, and public libraries. If you decide to gather information about owning a business, contact these sources. In addition, talk to other small-business owners about their experiences, joys, problems, mistakes, and successes. You may want to file your notes in your portfolio.

One in three new businesses fails within six months. Proper planning is key. A thorough business plan that addresses financing, marketing, and expanding your operation is a must. You will also benefit from completing an assessment for entrepreneurship or franchise ownership. Free assessments are available on the Internet. One example is http://www.2h.com/Tests/entrepreneur.html.

The following worksheet lists attributes that might indicate you would do well working for yourself. If you find that many of the statements apply to you, perhaps you should explore starting a business (becoming an entrepreneur) or providing a service using your special skills (becoming a freelancer).

I Consider Working for Myself

The statements I've checked are ones that apply to me.

____ I have a great idea for a new product or service.

____ I don't mind taking financial risks.

____ I like to work hard on a project in which I believe.

____ I like being in charge of things and taking all the responsibility for success and failure.

____ I am creative, flexible, and open to new ideas.

____ I am a self-starter, with a lot of self-discipline.

____ I can commit myself 100 percent to meeting deadlines.

____ I like working alone.

____ I can do whatever it takes to get the job done, no matter how many hours it takes.

____ I have financial management skills.

____ I like setting my own schedule.

____ I can set and keep work priorities.

____ I am able to motivate myself and others when I believe in what I am doing.

____ I work well with others even if I have just met them.

____ I am able to convince others about my point of view.

My business idea: _____

_____

_____

_____

▶ *LET'S REVIEW*

Place a check mark beside each statement that describes you. Review information in this chapter that applies to any statements you are unable to check.

Self-Assessment Checklist

_____ I can identify what would be an ideal job for me.

_____ I am familiar with several sources of career information.

_____ I know what kinds of questions to ask in an informational interview.

_____ I can define the word *networking.*

_____ I understand the importance of finding and enlisting people to be in my network.

_____ I know how to record information I've found about careers I'm interested in.

_____ I can identify community resources that offer or support education and training.

_____ I can identify and use information resources that give me details about occupations.

_____ I know what skills are necessary for self-employment.

Date: _____

Chapter 6

Deciding on a Career Direction

You've been making decisions for a long time. Some of your decisions may have been small in comparison to deciding your life's work. This chapter begins a discussion of a step-by-step model for making career decisions. The information here will help you answer these questions:

- What are the steps involved in making a career decision?
- How does what I know about myself influence the career decisions I make?
- What sources are available to help me consider various careers?
- What jobs most closely match my idea of the perfect job?
- What one career option do I want to pursue now?

People make career decisions in various ways. Some choose careers based on the advice of others. Some take the first job that comes along. Others choose an occupation because they have heard that there are many openings in a certain job area or industry. Sometimes decisions made this way turn out well. Other times they do not. Many working adults say they would choose differently if they had to do it over again—and they would definitely get more information before making a decision.

You, on the other hand, are spending time and thought on who you are and what you want. You are gathering information about career possibilities. Now you are ready to review your choices and make some decisions.

You may want to include in your portfolio some of the worksheets in this chapter. They should be included for your reference only.

Childhood Dreams

For some people, choosing a career is a difficult decision. Others know at an early age what career path they want to take. Actor Raymond Burr once said,

> *"The policeman is the little boy who grew up to be what he said he was going to be."*

Over the course of our lives, when we think about what we want to be, most of us change our minds several times. Think back to your childhood, when your knowledge about careers was limited. The following worksheet will help you think back about what you wanted to be when you grew up.

When I Was a Child

When I was a child, I wanted to be _____

_____

_____

The job sounded interesting to me because _____

_____

_____

These factors influenced me: _____

_____

_____

_____ My decision changed over the years. Here's why.

_____

_____

_____

_____ My decision never changed. Here's why.

_____

_____

_____

Career Decision-Making Model

You're no longer a child. You are faced with the reality of having to make career-related decisions. For big or complicated decisions like choosing your life's work, it helps to have a system for making decisions. Making satisfying decisions is a learning process—there is no magic formula. But there are ways to organize your thoughts and feelings to help you make sensible choices. Numerous methods and models are available that can help you.

The model shown below is a wheel tracing the basic steps to take when making decisions. If you start with *Decide to Decide* and follow each step, you can chart a course that will help you achieve your career and life goals. In this chapter, you will learn more about the first five steps on the model.

> For big or complicated decisions like choosing your life's work, it helps to have a system for making decisions.

A Model for Career Decision Making

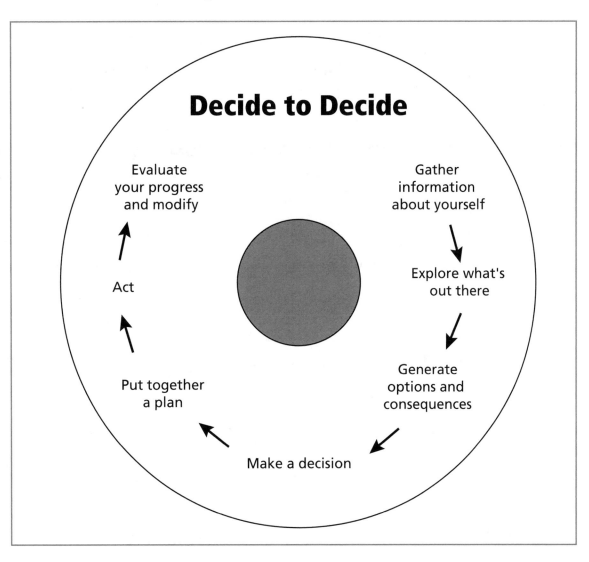

Decide to Decide

Tip Remember that no external factors can keep you from deciding to decide. Evaluate your current situation and determine what is best for you.

We all have a tendency to put off doing things. Sometimes we face conflicts or confrontation. Sometimes we feel we just don't have the time. Sometimes we simply don't want to do whatever it is we're putting off doing. However difficult, do not put off making a decision about something as important as your career.

Here's an example of how you might put off deciding to make a career change. Suppose you are laid off in the summer. You may think that this is a period when there is no hiring. And you would be partially correct. Summer has historically been a slow time for the economy. However, this is also a great time for networking, planting seeds, doing research, and building strategies. If you postpone your career change process, you are likely to have a hard time starting again. The time is lost and can't be recovered.

Remember that no external factors can keep you from deciding to decide. If you have a sincere desire to make a career decision, you already have the motivation to take this first step. The worksheet that follows asks you to put into words what you hope to accomplish by making a career decision. Remember, there are no right or wrong reasons for wanting to make a career decision:

- You may want more time to spend at home with your family.
- You may want a position that pays more or offers more benefits.
- You may want more long-term job security.
- You may want more or less involvement with people.

Evaluate your current situation and determine what is best for you. The only way you can do that is by knowing and listening to yourself. If you have completed the worksheets in the previous chapters of this book, you already have a good idea about who you are. Now is the time to decide what you want. Complete each sentence below, including as much information about your decision as possible.

I Decide to Decide

The career decision I'm ready to make: _____

_____

The reason I want to make this decision: _____

_____

When I want to see the results of my decision: _____

Gather Information About Yourself

As you have worked through this book, you have spent considerable time getting to know more about yourself. You may have learned something new or gained a new perspective. Maybe this self-examination was just a refresher course of what you knew but had forgotten. Maybe your self-examination revealed lots of information, but you just can't seem to make sense of it all.

> Getting to know yourself is like a journey—the destination is not as significant as what happens along the way.

Getting to know yourself is like a journey—the destination is not as significant as what happens along the way. Do not be alarmed if the pieces of the puzzle don't automatically fall into place.

> *"I wonder if I've been changed in the night? Let me think: was I the same when I got up this morning? I almost think I can remember feeling a little different. But if I'm not the same, the next question is, 'Who in the world am I?' Ah, that's the great puzzle!"*
>
> —Lewis Carroll, *Alice's Adventures in Wonderland*

Sorting It All Out

Sorting out all the information you've collected about yourself may take some time. Analyzing the information and determining how to apply your newfound knowledge may take even more time. Your self-knowledge is your foundation. This knowledge is applicable to every aspect of your life. The more you know about yourself, the better equipped you are to make choices that will bring you greater satisfaction.

> The more you know about yourself, the better equipped you are to make choices that will bring you greater satisfaction.

Perhaps the most difficult part of gathering information about yourself is that you must take a clear, honest look at who you are. If you are unable to confront a certain aspect of your life because it evokes unpleasant memories, perhaps you aren't being totally honest with yourself.

Be aware that issues you are unable to face do not go away simply because you choose not to face them. One approach you can take to confront these issues is to keep a journal. Discipline yourself to write about what you don't want to face. Perhaps you could talk with a member of your family, a close and trusted friend, a clergy member, or a professional counselor. Many sources of help are available to you in your local community. While the results of such in-depth introspection may be painful, the process may help you gain valuable information about yourself and your abilities. Perhaps you will even learn that you are stronger than you imagined.

Throughout your life, you will continually discover more about yourself. As you grow and learn, take time to examine your thoughts, feelings, actions, and reactions. Periodically, look at the worksheets in your portfolio and see how your perspectives, attitudes, values, and beliefs have changed or remained the same.

Knowing Yourself

All decisions start with the question, "What do I want?" In previous chapters of this book, you gathered personal information such as what you value and what you have to offer in terms of skills and experiences. You also thought about the barriers that can keep you from reaching your goals, and you examined your work and life achievements.

> All decisions start with the question, "What do I want?"

Now, use the following worksheet to review your work history. List what you liked and disliked about each of your past and present jobs.

My Likes and Dislikes

	What I Liked	What I Disliked
Current or most recent position		
Previous position		
Position prior to that		

Explore What's Out There

To make informed and responsible career decisions, you need reliable information about the opportunities available. Chapter 5 introduced you to some career exploration activities. You now should have some career possibilities in mind that you would like to explore further. Even after you are established in a career, your situation may change. You may find yourself exploring career options again. As you explore other options, don't underestimate the value of up-to-date and reliable career information.

> Even after you are established in a career, your situation may change. You may find yourself exploring career options again. Don't underestimate the value of up-to-date and reliable career information.

One good source for determining labor market information is the Bureau of Labor Statistics, U.S. Department of Labor (DOL). Its Web site is www.dol.gov. The bureau is responsible for publishing a variety of bulletins, articles, periodicals, and books that highlight current labor market trends. Be sure you interpret these trends accurately and do not overreact. Think about how certain trends may affect your situation positively or negatively. Here are some trends reflected in the DOL's most recent *Occupational Outlook Handbook:*

- Education and earnings are related. Many jobs can be obtained without a college degree, but most better-paying jobs require either training beyond high school or substantial work experience.

- Knowledge of computer and other technologies is increasingly important. In all fields, people without job-related technical and computer skills will have a more difficult time finding good opportunities than people who have these skills.

- Ongoing education and training are essential. Upgrading work-related skills on an ongoing basis is no longer optional for most jobs. People without technical or computer skills must get them.

- Good career planning has increased in importance. Most people will change their jobs many times and make major career changes five to seven times. Career-planning and job-seeking skills are the keys to surviving in this new economy.

Remember that this information applies to the general labor force. You must decide how to apply it to your situation.

Evaluate Options and Consequences

Tip Every action you take has consequences. The key to positive consequences is to think before you act or make a decision.

You may have many career choices to consider after exploring your options, but you also will have many career consequences. Every action you take has consequences. Sometimes the consequences are negative. For example, you might hit a baseball and break a window. Sometimes the consequences are positive. For example, you might hit a baseball and score a home run.

You cannot predict every consequence for every action, and many consequences are beyond your control. The key to positive consequences is to think before you act, or before you make a decision. Try to anticipate the outcome of your actions. One way to do that is to learn as much as you can about the action you are considering. Think about possible outcomes. If you can't live with the possible bad results, consider what you can do to ensure that the results are good. Also, remember that in every situation you do have control of your attitudes and reactions. You can choose to have a positive attitude or a negative attitude toward any consequence.

You also have at least some control over your circumstances. If you have completed the exercises in this book, you are armed with the knowledge to make better choices, which will result in better consequences.

"One of the great paradoxes of human development is that we are required to make crucial choices (about careers and work) before we have the knowledge, judgment, and self-understanding to choose wisely. Yet if we put off these choices until we feel truly ready, the delay may produce other and greater costs."

—Daniel J. Levinson, Psychologist, *Seasons of a Man's Life*

You have hopefully discovered by now that you have many choices and options. One of the most difficult parts of decision making is sorting out and narrowing your options. How do you know which ones to pick? The following Career Options Grid gives you a place to start.

Career Options Grid

On the following page is a career options grid. As you complete the grid, you will compare information about yourself to information about career possibilities. You may be considering new career options, or you may want to move your current career in a new direction. Perhaps you have decided you want to stay in the same occupation but consider a new job. As you complete the following worksheet, ask yourself these questions about your career options:

- Does this career option involve tasks and responsibilities that interest me?

- Does it require the skills I have or would like to develop?

- Is the work schedule and environment suitable for me?

- Do I have the required training or education?

- Will this career option provide an adequate income for me?

- How many new jobs will be available in this occupation?

- Does this career option match my values, temperament, and the amount of risk I want to take?

- Do I have disabilities that would get in the way of doing the work?

- How does this career option fit in with what I picture for my future?

Look at the following worksheet. Here's how the grid works:

1. Down the left side of the grid are work and personal characteristics.

2. The first column at the top is labeled "Ideal Job." In this column, every work and personal characteristic is checked, because your ideal job would be what you are looking for in each area.

3. In the other columns across the top, list career options you are considering.

4. In the column below each career option, check the characteristics that the option has in common with your ideal job, as far as providing what you want.

5. Put a slash (/) in the box if the option is only partly compatible with what you want.

6. Leave the space blank if the option doesn't fit at all.

My Career Options Grid

	Ideal Job	Option 1:	Option 2:	Option 3:	Option 4:	Option 5:
Work Characteristics						
Advancement	X					
Coworkers	X					
Earnings	X					
Location	X					
Outlook	X					
Physical demands	X					
Responsibilities	X					
Risks	X					
Tasks	X					
Work environment	X					
Workload	X					
Work pace	X					
Work schedule	X					
Personal Characteristics						
Accomplishments	X					
Career values	X					
Decision-making style	X					
Education and training	X					
Emotional health	X					
Life roles	X					
Life values	X					
Learning style	X					
Nonwork experience	X					
Personality style	X					
Physical health	X					
Risk-taking style	X					
Skills	X					
Stress-management style	X					
Time-management style	X					
Work experience	X					

Reviewing Your Career Options Grid

 Tip Determine which positive and negative consequences are most important to you.

Review what you have checked under each career option you wrote in at the top of the grid. Rank them according to how well they match your work and personal characteristics. Judge what is most important to you. Are earnings more important than an agreeable work environment? Is having a good work schedule more important than getting to use your skills? Is the job outlook more important than your values? Which options suit you best? Narrow your choices to the top two options.

Now consider what might happen if you choose one of those two careers. What might be the consequences of your decision? Can you live with those consequences? How would your decision change your life? Think of both positive and negative outcomes. A negative consequence does not mean you should disregard that option. But you should determine which positive and negative consequences are most important to you.

On the following worksheet, list the two career options you chose as the best match for you according to the Career Options Grid. Use words, pictures, or symbols to describe the positive and negative things that may happen as a result of your decisions.

My Top Two Career Choices

Of the careers I've considered, the two I think most closely match my idea of the perfect job are

1. _____

2. _____

Some possible positive and negative consequences of these two options are

1. _____

_____

_____

_____

_____

2. _____

_____

_____

_____

_____

Make a Decision

You have completed the first four steps of the Career Decision-Making Model. Now, you are ready to make a decision.

> *"Some problems are so complex that you have to be highly intelligent and well informed just to be undecided about them."*
>
> —Laurence J. Peter, *Peter's Almanac*

Making a decision is difficult. When faced with a decision, you can think of all kinds of possibilities, but just thinking about the possibilities doesn't make them a reality.

Evaluating your decisions is an important part of the process and should not be overlooked. One common misconception is that there are only good and bad decisions. In reality, there are only satisfying and unsatisfying decisions. And you are the only one who can determine if your decisions are satisfying or unsatisfying.

> One common misconception is that there are only good and bad decisions. In reality, there are only satisfying and unsatisfying decisions. And you are the only one who can determine if your decisions are satisfying or unsatisfying.

Make a commitment to your decisions. What can you do to follow through on your decisions? Maybe you need to prioritize all the activities in your life so your career comes out on top. Perhaps what you want seems too far-fetched because you're looking at the big picture. Sometimes breaking things down into a series of attainable goals produces a more realistic and clear picture. Commitment to making your decision a reality means focusing your energies on a new course of action. You must adapt to a new situation, career, or lifestyle.

Be aware of how you feel after you make your decision. Are you excited about the possibilities that await you? Are you apprehensive? Are you afraid of the outcome? Are you just relieved to have made a decision—any decision? Are you confident that you made the best choice available for you?

Remember that feeling apprehensive or scared doesn't mean you made the wrong choice. Those feelings are normal reactions to change. However, if you are feeling more anxiety than contentment, you may want to review the information under "Self-Management Style" in Chapter 3.

Also, remember that no decision is final; you can always change your mind and revise your decision. Just be sure you stick with your decision long enough to objectively evaluate your progress and make necessary modifications. In time, you may feel perfectly comfortable with a decision that you felt quite apprehensive about at first.

If you are having trouble deciding what you want, don't feel bad. You don't have to map out the rest of your life. The purpose is to start planning for the next few years. This decision-making process can help you lay a foundation for your future and give you an advantage in the job market—one that you can use time and time again if necessary.

In the following worksheet, choose the career option you will pursue. Refer to the previous worksheet called "My Top Two Career Choices." Base your choice on a combination of personal reasons and external factors. Check your feelings, your likes and dislikes, and the information you have about the career. Record your best career option and the reasons you think this is the best choice for you.

My Decision

Based on my Career Options Grid, the career I have chosen to pursue is

_____

My reasons for this decision:

_____

_____

_____

_____

My feelings about making this decision: _____

_____

_____

_____

_____

▶ *LET'S REVIEW*

Place a check mark beside each statement that describes you. Review information in this chapter that applies to any statements you are unable to check.

Self-Assessment Checklist

_____ I can describe the Career Decision-Making Model shown at the beginning of this chapter.

_____ I have decided to make a career decision.

_____ I know what I like and dislike about my current and past work experiences.

_____ I understand the importance of current career information when I make career-related decisions.

_____ I have compared several career options to my idea of the perfect job.

_____ I have chosen the two career options that most closely match my ideal job.

_____ I am aware of some possible positive and negative consequences of my career decisions.

_____ I have chosen the career option I will pursue at this time.

_____ I can explain why I choose that option.

_____ I can describe how I feel about my career decision.

Date: _____

Chapter 7

Getting and Keeping Your Job

In this chapter, you will finish the decision-making process you started in Chapter 6 using the Career Decision-Making Model. In that chapter, you identified some possible career targets. Now you will put together a plan for landing a job in the career area that interests you most. You also will find in this chapter some valuable information about keeping your job.

This chapter will help answer these questions:

- What actions do I need to take to make my dreams a reality?
- What tools and information will I need in my job search?
- When I am offered a job, how can I decide if it's the right job for me?
- After I find a job, what can I do to help ensure that I keep my job and continue to improve as an employee?

You are well on your way to finding the right job for you. When you complete this chapter, you will have the confidence and knowledge needed for finding and keeping a job. For your own reference, you may want to include some of the worksheets in this chapter in your portfolio.

Put Together a Plan

> **Tip** Keep in mind that there is no best way to find a job. The best way is the way that works for you.

The last three steps in the Career Decision-Making Model require action. The following exercises will help you get started on your job search and will make you aware of some essential tools such as resumes and cover letters. Many methods are available that can help you find a job, but your success ultimately depends on how much time and energy you are willing to invest in your search. Keep in mind that there is no *best* way to find a job. The best way is the way that works for you.

Once you've made your decision, it's time to *do* something about it. The decision becomes your goal—a target for your actions.

You want to do more than just dreaming about what you want to do. You want to put together a plan of action that will help make your dreams a reality. Action planning involves deciding what you will do and when you will do it.

On the following worksheet, write your goal and list what you must do to accomplish your goal. Give yourself a deadline for each step. What do you need to do today, tomorrow, next week? Make your deadlines reasonable, but don't allow yourself time to get sidetracked. After writing down the steps and completion dates, sign your plan and date it.

Next, share your completed worksheet with someone else. This is a way of making the commitment to carry out the steps and keep yourself on schedule. Find someone who will be supportive of your plans and who can encourage you as you go along. Tell this person about your deadlines and ask him or her to check with you on your progress. You may want to have this person sign and date the worksheet. Knowing that someone will be monitoring your progress motivates you to get things done.

Check your plan often as a reminder. Use another sheet of paper if you need more space.

My Plan of Action

My goal: _____

_____

_____

I will take the following steps to reach this goal.

First step: _____ Deadline date:_____

Second step:_____ Deadline date:_____

Third step:_____ Deadline date:_____

Fourth step: _____ Deadline date:_____

Fifth step: _____ Deadline date:_____

_____ I understand that this is my plan and that I have a responsibility to myself to complete it and to review and update it regularly.

Signature _____ Date _____

I have shared this plan with _____

Signature _____ Date _____

Act

Making a decision and putting together a plan aren't enough to make your decision real. You have to take action. The actions you take will depend on the steps you have listed in your plan. For example, the next step in your career plan might be to look for a job or to develop new skills.

> A dream can become a reality—but only if you take action to make it so.

Perhaps training or education is your next step. The key to reaching your goal is to follow your plan and to modify and add to it as needed. Take the steps one at a time and finish each one according to plan. A dream can become a reality—but only if you take action to make it so.

If you are looking for a job, you will need certain tools. The following sections describe some of those tools.

Job Applications

You will fill out applications before interviews or during the hiring process. Often, your job application gives employers their first look at you. How you fill out a job application reveals whether you have the following important characteristics:

> Your job application gives employers their first look at you.

1. **The ability to prepare and think ahead.** Secretaries and receptionists have many stories to tell about unprepared applicants who ask for pens, pencils, and telephone books. They often give out several applications because job seekers make mistakes filling them out. Do receptionists tell the interviewer about these people? You bet they do! Be prepared!

   When you visit a place of employment to fill out a job application or interview for a job, take a copy of the following worksheet called "My Job Application Fact Sheet" and at least two pens and pencils. Also take a copy of your resume to submit with the application or to leave with the employer (more on resumes in the following section).

2. **The ability to follow instructions and to use accurate information.** Every job requires you to read, understand, and follow written instructions, rules, or procedures. Be sure you fill out the job application correctly.

   Read the entire application before you start to fill it out. Make sure you understand the instructions in each section. Follow the instructions exactly. If the application says to print, then print your information. Leave blank any section that says, "For employer's use only" or "Do not write below this line." Some applications ask you to list your most recent job first; others want the list in the reverse order. Read carefully.

   Be honest. If you are hired for the job and your employer discovers that you have intentionally lied on the application, you will likely be terminated.

3. **The ability to complete a document neatly and to follow through on a task.** Crossed-out or poorly erased information gives a negative impression that reflects on the quality of your work.

   Be careful not to leave any sections or lines in the application blank. Avoid writing "see above" or "see resume." Fill out the information requested. If you don't, the employer may assume you will not follow through on the details of a job. Of course, some questions may not apply to you. For these questions, put "N/A" (non-applicable) in the space.

You can use the following worksheet to organize the information you need for filling out applications. Complete the form and take it with you as a reference when you fill out a job application or have an interview. As you completed previous chapters in this book, you gathered most of the information called for on this worksheet. Refer back to those worksheets now.

My Job Application Fact Sheet

Identification

Name _____

Street address _____

City _____ State _____ ZIP _____

Phone_____ E-mail _____

Social Security number _____ Driver's license number_____

Name and telephone number of a person to contact in an emergency _____

Type of job desired/Job requirements_____

_____

_____

Name of position I am applying for_____

Date available to begin work _____ Salary or pay rate expected _____

Previous Employment

Job title _____

Employer_____

Street address _____

City _____ State _____ ZIP _____

Phone_____ Fax _____

Dates employed _____ Reason for leaving _____

Special skills demonstrated _____

_____

_____

Job title _____

Employer_____

Street address _____

City _____ State _____ ZIP _____

Phone_____ Fax _____

Dates employed _____ Reason for leaving _____

Special skills demonstrated _____

_____

_____

Job title _____

Employer_____

Street address _____

City _____ State _____ ZIP _____

Phone_____ Fax _____

Dates employed _____ Reason for leaving _____

Special skills demonstrated _____

_____

_____

Formal Education

School most recently attended _____

Address _____

Dates attended _____ Degree earned _____

Activities, honors, clubs, sports _____

_____

School _____

Address _____

Dates attended _____ Degree earned _____

Activities, honors, clubs, sports _____

_____

References

Name _____

Street address _____

City _____ State _____ ZIP _____

Phone_____ E-mail _____

Relationship (employer, teacher, coworker, clergy) _____

Name _____

Street address _____

City _____ State _____ ZIP _____

Phone_____ E-mail _____

Relationship (employer, teacher, coworker, clergy) _____

Name _____

Street address _____

City _____ State _____ ZIP _____

Phone_____ E-mail _____

Relationship (employer, teacher, coworker, clergy) _____

Resumes

By working through the previous chapters in this book, you have already done much of the work needed to put together or update your resume. Employers want more than a list of job duties or where you worked and when. They are interested in how well you did your job, what skills and experience you have to offer, your strengths, and what you accomplished. Review the worksheets in previous chapters to identify information you want to include in your resume.

Also look through the other documents you have filed in your portfolio. Review educational records, training certificates, and letters of recommendation or performance evaluations for information you may want in your resume.

> Employers want more than a list of job duties or where you worked and when. They are interested in how well you did your job, what skills and experience you have to offer, your strengths, and what you accomplished.

The goal of writing a resume is to include just enough information to get an interview with the employer. Save the detailed information for the interview. Think of a resume as an advertisement you use to get an interview.

Your resume should be

- Free of spelling, punctuation, grammar, or keyboard errors
- Short, concise, and specific
- Appealing to the eye and printed on quality paper

It should

- Emphasize your accomplishments and how you can benefit the employer
- Highlight the skills and strengths you have that relate to your target job

There are many ways to put a resume together. Remember the following points:

1. **The most effective resume is one that focuses on the requirements of the job.** Customize your resume. You may need two or three versions of your resume if you are applying for different kinds of jobs.

   Use the same basic information in each version of your resume. Arrange and emphasize your skills, abilities, strengths, and background information differently to match the requirements of each job.

   This can be a difficult task, but it will be easier if you use a computer with a word-processing program. If you don't have access to a computer, consider having your resume prepared by someone who does have one—a professional resume writer or a friend or family member. Find someone who will not mind changing the resume as needed.

   Another option is to customize your resume cover letter to list the most important information about you that matches each job's requirements (more about cover letters in the following section).

2. **Your most important assets—the information you want to be sure the employer reads—should be highlighted near the top of your resume.** The top half of the first page of your resume is referred to as the "prime space" of your resume. The information in this area is what the employer will read first. It should contain the information that is most important for the employer to see. As you write your resume, ask yourself what information you most want an employer to see when considering you for a specific job.

   You might want an employer to know about your current or most recent job or about your recent training. You might want the employer to have a summary of your education, experience, skills and strengths, or achievements. Choose what is most important for the particular job. Place this information in the prime space on your resume.

3. **Your name, address, and phone number should appear at the top of the resume.** Use bold lettering or divide the sections of your resume with lines to make it easier to read. You also may want to use bold type or underline the highlights of your resume. This might include the names of the companies for which you have worked and your dates of employment. Bold or underlined type allows a prospective employer to scan the page and immediately see this information.

Keep copies of your resumes in your portfolio so you can refer to them in the future. Updating or rearranging an old resume is easier than starting over.

Use the following worksheet as a guide for assembling the essential elements of your resume. After you have the information together, try various formats until you have a design that is functional and agreeable. Refer to worksheets you completed in previous chapters.

My Resume Worksheet

Name _____

Address _____

Telephone _____

E-mail _____

Summary

Here's a description of who I am, what industry knowledge I have, my marketable skills and attributes, and how I can benefit the company and the employer: _____

_____

_____

_____

_____

_____

The kind of position I want is _____

_____

_____

_____

Education and Training

My recent education and training: _____

_____

_____

_____

How this education and training matches my job target: _____

_____

_____

_____

_____

Current or Most Recent Job

_____

_____

List of Skills

_____

_____

_____

_____

List of Achievements and Outcomes

_____

_____

_____

_____

Summary of Experience

_____

_____

_____

_____

Qualification Highlights

_____

_____

_____

_____

Previous Employment

_____

_____

_____

_____

Additional Education and Training

_____

_____

_____

_____

Cover Letters

Tip

If you send your resume with a cover letter that is hurriedly prepared and that contains even one conspicuous error, all of your effort on your resume will be wasted.

In the past, most cover letters merely told the employer where the applicant heard about the job and indicated that a resume was attached. Today's cover letter is used for a variety of purposes.

You will want to spend a lot of time and effort ensuring that your resume is perfect —and rightly so. But if you send your resume with a cover letter that is hurriedly prepared and that contains even one conspicuous error, all of your effort on your resume will be wasted.

Your cover letter

- Shows a link between you and another person the employer already knows

- Describes your interest in the job

- Indicates your knowledge of the organization

- Lists additional information not included in your resume

- Emphasizes your skills, background, and strengths and shows how they match the job requirements

- Explains any special circumstances

- Indicates your interest in being interviewed

To be effective, your cover letter should

- Be free of spelling, punctuation, grammar, or keyboard errors

- Use a standard business letter format printed on quality paper

- Be addressed to a specific individual by name and title, if possible

Keep your cover letter short (one page) and make sure it is easy to read. Avoid long paragraphs. Use short lists. If you are unsure about proper spelling and grammar, refer to a dictionary. Ask someone who has good writing skills to proofread your cover letter.

Your cover letter is the perfect opportunity to deliver customized communication to your prospective employer. It introduces the employer to your resume and draws attention to information you want to highlight. Use your network to get the name of a person to contact. Address your cover letter to that person. If you are persistent and creative, you will find the contact you need.

> Your cover letter is the perfect opportunity to deliver customized communication to your prospective employer.

The following sample cover letter can serve as a guide for you as you write your cover letter.

Sara N. Wrap

7 High Street
Haverhill, MA 01850
Telephone: 978-374-5555
E-mail: saranwrap@aol.com

January 1, XXXX
Mr. Robert L. Smith
Vice President, Smith Industries
123 Market Street
Sellersburg, IN 11122

Dear Mr. Smith:

As a professional with five years experience in marketing, research, sales, and management, I am writing in regard to your Marketing Communications Manager position.

I am sure you will agree that my extensive and related experience makes me the ideal candidate to market Lawrence Memorial Hospital, as the following chart demonstrates.

Your Requirements	My Qualifications
Marketing experience	Extensive experience developing marketing plans from concept to implementation to evaluation
Ability to control research	Over 10 years' experience doing direct marketing research and serving in a supervisory and analytical capacity
Coordinate promotional and advertising campaigns	Developed and coordinated advertising and promotional campaigns for two organizations, developing the concepts and coordinating all resources
Knowledge of healthcare industry	Extensive firsthand knowledge of healthcare learned through previous employment

As requested, I have enclosed my resume with further details of my qualifications and accomplishments. I look forward to meeting with you to discuss how I may fit into your organization, add value to your professional staff, and lead your marketing functions. I will call you early next week to see if we might set a mutually convenient time to get together.

Sincerely,

Sara N. Wrap

Follow the format of the example to compose your own, personalized cover letter in the following worksheet.

My Cover Letter Outline

(my name) _____

(street address) _____

(city, state, ZIP) _____

(phone number) _____

(other contact information) _____

(date) _____

(employer's name) _____

(employer's job title, company name)_____

(street address) _____

(city, state, ZIP) _____

Dear (employer's title and last name) _____

(paragraph stating what I know about the company or industry and telling the name of a referral if I have one) _____

_____

_____

(general statement of what I know about the position and why I am well suited to the position) _____

_____

_____

(more specific description of the skills, abilities, and strengths I bring to the position— a chart or paragraph) _____

_____

_____

(concluding paragraph that states when and how I will follow up, requests an interview, and says thank-you) _____

_____

_____

Sincerely,

(my signature) _____

(my printed name) _____

Employer Contacts

In Chapter 5, you completed a diagram to show who you might contact for career information. Those same individuals can help you in your job search by providing employer contacts and information about job openings. The goal is to expand your network so that you have many sources of information. One great, inexpensive way of expanding your network is to let your fingers do the walking!

You will find that most people will want to help you if you make it easy for them. Do your homework first and remember that by accepting help you are obligated to give help to others in your network when the time comes.

Many job seekers say that making telephone inquiries is a difficult thing for them to do. If you are one of those people, having a telephone script can help. A script should include the following information:

- A greeting
- Your name
- The name of the contact person who suggested that you call
- The purpose of your call
- Two or three things about you that will interest the employer
- A request for a face-to-face meeting

If you still find yourself uncomfortable calling a stranger about job openings, start by making one or more practice calls to people you know. This will prepare you for calling people you do not know.

Sometimes an employer insists on interviewing you over the phone. This is a good thing. Keep your resume at hand to help you remember what you want to say about yourself. If you call an employer who decides to interview you on the phone right then, send the employer your resume and a thank-you letter as a follow up.

When you are on the telephone, make sure you stand up straight. This allows the diaphragm to expand fully and will improve the tone of your voice, lower the pitch, and make your voice sound warmer.

The following worksheet will help you develop a phone script. When you have completed this exercise, practice speaking your script aloud. Keep refining your script until you are comfortable speaking it and the words feel natural.

Be sure your script is not too long. You want to sell yourself without sounding like a telemarketer. That means you need to get across all your vital information in the first 30 seconds or so. Time yourself when you practice saying your script aloud.

To conclude the phone call, ask when you can come in for an interview. Do not ask *if* you can come in but *when* you can come in. Make it hard for the employer to turn you down. After all, your goal is to get an interview. Fill in the following worksheet to help organize your thoughts and create your personalized phone script.

> Do not ask *if* you can come in but *when* you can come in. Make it hard for the employer to turn you down.

My Telephone Script

Good morning. My name is _____

I'm calling at the suggestion of (name of referral)_____,
a business acquaintance of yours. He/she said you might know of an opening in your
organization or another organization for a person of my abilities.

I have over _____ years of experience in (description of the skills, abilities, and strengths
I can contribute to the organization; information about how well I perform my tasks
and responsibilities) _____

_____

_____

_____

_____

When would be a good time for me to come in for an interview?

Interviews

The more you prepare for an interview, the better you do. The two key steps to
preparing for interviews are finding out about the employer and practicing the
interview.

Finding Out About the Employer

Employers like applicants who take the time to get
information about the job and the company. If
you have this kind of information, you let the
employer know that you have selected the job and
the company carefully. The background information you gather before the interview will help you
decide whether the job and organization fit you.
This information is available through the following resources:

> Employers like applicants
> who take the time to get
> information about the job
> and the company.

- People in your network or people who work for the company where you will be
  interviewing

- Job postings

- Company brochures

- Company Web sites

- The company's competition, vendors, and customers

- Reference materials in your local library, particularly periodicals

- Public or private placement services

Practicing the Interview

> **Tip** If you cannot communicate your skills and abilities to an employer, you probably will not get the job. Practice can help.

If you cannot communicate your skills and abilities to an employer, you probably will not get the job. Practice can help. Many employers ask standard questions in an interview. The questions generally fall into a few categories such as work history and experience, strengths and weaknesses, goals, education or training history, and how you fit the job and the organization.

Many job-seeking books or government pamphlets contain lists of frequently asked interview questions. Find a list and practice answering the questions. Spend more time on the ones that seem hard to answer. Sometimes schools, colleges or universities, or job training agencies have workshops on interviewing.

Here are some additional tips to remember:

- Arrive at the interview early.

- Know what is in your resume and bring an extra copy.

- Think about how you can solve the employer's problem and benefit the company.

- Go into the interview with a positive attitude.

- Give complete but concise answers to the questions.

- Do not make negative comments about previous employers or coworkers.

- Keep your remarks targeted to the job. Sometimes even an interviewer gets off the subject, but try to remain focused on the matter at hand.

- Leave personal concerns at home so they do not hinder your chances.

- Do not bring up salary or compensation. Let the employer do this. Remember that the first person who talks about money loses.

The questions on the following worksheet are ones employers frequently ask. Get ready for your next interview by answering these questions. If you have completed the other worksheets in this book, you should be able to answer these questions.

Write the answers on the worksheet or record them on an audio- or videotape. Practice in front of a mirror or with a friend who will give you good advice. If you can, find someone who has hiring and interviewing experience. This person can tell you what you're doing right and where you could improve.

The questions in the worksheet are ones an employer might ask you. Record what you would say in response to each question.

> You must find a way to be positive about your previous work experiences and forget about the negatives when you are interviewing. This is important even if you have deep-seated resentment against an employer who fired you or treated you badly.

My Practice Interview Questions

Employer's Question	My Answer

Employer's Question

1. Tell me something about yourself.

2. Why are you interested in this job?

3. What kind of work have you been doing?

4. What would previous employers say about you?

5. What are your strongest skills and how have you used them?

6. What are your weaknesses and what would you like to improve about yourself?

7. What have you learned from previous jobs?

8. What is your most significant work experience?

9. Why should I hire you for this job?

My Answer

1. _____
_____
_____
_____

2. _____
_____
_____
_____

3. _____
_____
_____
_____

4. _____
_____
_____
_____

5. _____
_____
_____
_____

6. _____
_____
_____
_____

7. _____
_____
_____

8. _____
_____
_____

9. _____
_____
_____
_____

Follow Up

Many employers say that the way a person searches for work tells them what kind of an employee the person will be. Employers would rather give the job to someone who really wants it than to someone who does not seem to care. By following up after making a contact or having an interview, you show the employer how eager you are to get the job.

Consider the following:

- You may be the only applicant who takes the time to write a follow-up letter or make a phone call.

- Your follow-up is an opportunity to tell the employer something you may have forgotten to mention in the interview.

> Employers would rather give the job to someone who really wants it than to someone who does not seem to care.

- The employer may have several job openings. If you are not right for one, you may be right for another. Your follow-up gives an employer a reason to take another look at you.

- If the employer is not interested in you, always ask for the name of someone else you can contact for job leads. This will give you power and hope and may lead you to your next job.

- Always follow up within 24 to 48 hours after the interview.

Job Offers

Looking for work is difficult. After interviewing for a job, make your decision carefully. Getting an offer does not necessarily mean you should take the job. Most employers will not expect you to make a decision on the spot. You will probably be given a week or more to make up your mind. Instead of making a decision on impulse, carefully weigh the advantages and disadvantages of the job. This helps ensure that you make an informed decision.

> Getting an offer does not necessarily mean you should take the job. Most employers will not expect you to make a decision on the spot.

Evaluating Job Offers

There are some general parameters you should follow when evaluating job offers. Consider these questions:

- Do the employer's values match your own?

- What was your initial impression of the company and its employees?

- Do the employees you met seem like people you would like to work with on a regular basis?

- Do the employees seem interested and excited about their work?

On the following worksheet, check the aspects of this position that would match or come close to your idea of the perfect job. Refer to the "My Career Values" and "My Life Values" worksheets in Chapter 3 and to the "My Perfect Job" worksheet in Chapter 5. Base your responses on information you gained at the interview.

I Evaluate a Job Offer

The Job

_____ Duties and responsibilities

_____ Personalities, supervisors and colleagues

_____ Opportunity for achievement

_____ Opportunity to work independently

_____ Overtime

_____ Social significance of job

_____ Pressure and pace of work; turnover

_____ Values/interests/skills

_____ Variety of work assignments

_____ Exposure to outstanding colleagues

_____ Opportunity/frequency of travel

_____ Use of academic background

_____ Physical environment/ working conditions

_____ Intellectual stimulation

The Organization

_____ Technologically innovative

_____ Management style

_____ Layoffs and restructuring

_____ Financial stability and growth prospects

_____ People in top level positions

_____ Training and continuing education

_____ Public or private employer

_____ Involvement in research and design

_____ Growth and advancement

_____ Reputation and image of employer

_____ Salary and benefits

_____ Personnel policies and flex-time

_____ Required relocation and transfers

_____ Well established vs. fledging

The Industry

_____ Growth

_____ Dependence on government

_____ Long-term future potential

_____ Future needs for goods and services

_____ Dependence on business cycle

_____ Record of layoffs or downsizing

The Location

_____ Proximity of schools

_____ Climate

_____ Community life/environment

_____ Opportunities for family's careers

_____ Cost of living

_____ Location of company sites

Your Career and Life Plan Portfolio

Three Job Offer Options

After you interview for a job and receive a job offer, you can respond in various ways. Here are three options. You can

1. **Stall.** First and foremost, express appreciation for the offer. Tell the employer that because this is such an important decision you will need time to think about your decision carefully. Agree on a reasonable time frame for when you will make a final decision. Fortunately, most organizations will not expect you to accept an offer on the spot.

    If you decide to make a counteroffer, you only have one chance to do so. Know what you will do if the employer is not open to the terms of your offer. You can ask for what you want, but be prepared for the employer to say no.

2. **Accept the offer.** Show your appreciation for the offer. Ask the employer to confirm the offer in writing. Do not interview for any other positions. Reject all other offers by telephone and then with a short letter. Never renege on an offer you have already accepted.

3. **Reject the offer.** Express your appreciation for the offer and for the company's confidence in you. Say something positive about the employer and be diplomatic. Sending a follow-up letter is a professional way to conclude your interactions even if you have already expressed your appreciation verbally.

An Action Checklist

By working through the chapters in this book, you have already done much to prepare yourself to look for work. The information in the previous sections of this chapter gave you an idea of certain things you will need to do in your job search. Use the following checklist to keep track of what you have done and what you need to do.

You probably already know how to do many of the actions listed in the following worksheet. For each action, fill in a target date. Then check off each action as you complete it.

My Action Checklist

I will take the following actions to help me look for a job.

Action	Target Date	Completed
Contact employers, colleagues, and other persons to ask them to serve as references for me.		
Get letters of recommendation from my references.		
Talk with friends, family, business contacts, and other people to discuss potential employment contacts (networking).		
Update or prepare my resume.		
Prepare a cover letter.		
Plan how I will get to the employment interviews and job sites.		
Develop a telephone script for making initial inquiries.		
Call or write potential employers.		
Send letters and resumes to potential employers.		
Research employers with whom I want to interview.		
Practice my interviewing skills with friends, family, and other contacts.		
Maintain an active file on employment inquiry contacts.		
Follow up employment contacts with thank-you letters, telephone contacts, and/or more information about myself.		

Some important things I need to remember as I look for a job:

_____

_____

_____

_____

Evaluate Your Progress and Modify

Tip ▸ Don't lose sight of your goals. Make your decisions work for you.

By working through the worksheets provided previously in this book, you have completed seven of the eight steps in the Career Decision-Making Model shown in Chapter 6. The last step on the model is to evaluate the progress you have made toward your goal and modify your plan as needed.

> *"Make no little plans; they have no magic to stir men's blood and probably themselves will not be realized. Make big plans; aim high in hope and work."*

—Daniel H. Burnham

As you evaluate your progress, you may find you are on track. Or you may discover something about your plan, your situation, or yourself that has changed your goal or changed the steps necessary to get there. Remember that the plan and the decision are yours. You can evaluate and change them at any point.

Look again at the Career Decision-Making Model in Chapter 6 as you complete the following worksheet. If you need to review any of the steps, do so. Don't lose sight of your goals. Make your decisions work for you, even if you have to start over on the decision-making model using new information.

My Plan Is in Progress

What new pieces of information do I have about the career I decided to pursue? _____

_____

_____

_____

_____

Does this new information change my decision? In what way? _____

_____

_____

_____

_____

Have I reached my goal? If not, what is keeping me from progressing? _____

_____

_____

_____

_____

If I have reached my goal, am I ready to think about a new goal and start the decision-making process again? _____

_____

_____

_____

I will evaluate my progress again on the following date: _____

_____

Keep Your New Job

> **Tip** One of the biggest mistakes new workers make is not asking enough questions at the beginning and asking too many later on.

All the work you have done so far has been in an effort to find the job you want. So what do you do after you get the job? The first few days on the job are referred to as a honeymoon. This is because the employer is pleased to have you working and does not yet expect you to know everything about the workplace and the tasks of the job. During your first week on the job, you can take a step toward success. Show your interest in how the organization works. Get to know your supervisor and coworkers. Learn as much as you can about the job and your new work environment. Don't be afraid to ask questions. One of the biggest mistakes new workers make is not asking enough questions at the beginning and asking too many later on.

Remember to update your resume during your first week on the job. As you think about your long-term career management plan, make yourself visible and create a backup plan for what you will do if aspects of the job do not meet your expectations. Remember, you control your destiny.

The survival of an organization depends in great part on the quality of its workforce. Employers agree that the ability of an employee to keep a job depends on the worker's success in these five basic areas:

1. **Dependability and reliability.** Frequent absences or absences without good reasons are cause for dismissal. Employers rely on workers to follow through on tasks given them.

2. **Punctuality.** Employers expect their employees to report for work at the time agreed upon. Workers who are late at the start of work, late for meetings, or late returning from lunch or breaks delay the work of others and cause problems for coworkers, supervisors, and customers.

3. **Quality of work.** Employers depend on workers to produce a quality product or service. Not only is quality important in competing with other organizations that provide the same product or service, it is a key to company and job survival.

4. **Quantity of work.** Productivity is another important element in keeping a job. A successful worker is one who produces more than enough goods or services to justify his or her wage and who keeps costs down to help the organization make a profit.

5. **Interpersonal communication skills.** Employers do not want to hire new employees who are unable to get along with coworkers. An employee who causes problems or who does not treat fellow employees with respect and maturity puts the whole company at risk.

The following worksheet lists areas you should explore in the first week of your new job. Most of the information here can be provided by your supervisor. Remember to ask questions. Don't guess!

My First-Week Checklist

The checked items indicate what I've learned during the first week on my new job.
I've also made a few notes about things I want to remember.

Schedule

____ Work hours _____

____ Lunch hour _____

____ Break times _____

Organizational structure

____ Who supervises whom _____

____ Name of supervisor's boss _____

____ Name of supervisor _____

____ Names of coworkers _____

Pay

____ Frequency _____

____ Pay day _____

____ Method of payment _____

____ Benefits _____

____ Shift differential or overtime pay _____

Job

____ Job description _____

____ Detailed discussion of tasks and responsibilities _____

____ Work area _____

____ How my job fits into overall operation _____

____ Who to ask when I have questions _____

____ Evaluations: How? When? By whom? _____

Policies

____ Absences: Who to notify, number to call _____

____ Lateness _____

____ Security/Confidentiality _____

____ Smoking _____

____ Parking _____

Growing on the Job

The workplace of the future demands constant learning and growing. Employers expect more from their workers today than they have in the past. Global competition, changing technology, and the need for a highly skilled workforce make employers very careful about who they hire, who they keep, and who they promote. You will be a more valuable asset to your organization and will be happier with yourself if you keep learning new skills, taking more responsibilities, and identifying and pursuing new directions for your personal and professional growth.

> You will be a more valuable asset to your organization and will be happier with yourself if you keep learning new skills, taking more responsibilities, and identifying and pursuing new directions for your personal and professional growth.

Employers agree that in order to grow on the job employees should

- **Know how to learn.** Realize the importance of career-long learning and take advantage of on-the-job or after-work training.

- **Be able to read, write, and do computation.** Improve these skills, which are critical to learning new job functions.

- **Listen and communicate well.** Understand instructions and problems; communicate effectively with coworkers, supervisors, and customers.

- **Be flexible.** Adapt to changes in technology and in the job, solve problems in a creative way, and try new ideas and methods.

- **Be willing to work as part of a team.** Work effectively with others; lead when necessary; work with others who are different in gender, age, race, or cultural background.

- **Provide outstanding customer service.** Look for ways to improve relationships with customers and vendors.

- **Have good self-management skills.** Be a self-starter; be honest and ethical; take responsibility for your actions; look for ways to develop and improve skills and traits important to the job and the organization.

- **Be able to solve problems and think critically.** Always look at the root of the problem and how you can add value to the organization.

As you look at the characteristics included in the previous list, compare them to the skills you have. Review the worksheets you completed in Chapter 4. Ask yourself these questions:

- Do I have the skills needed to succeed in my job?

- Which skills can I improve?

- What actions can I take to improve my skills?

Read each statement on the following worksheet. In the right-hand columns, check the items you have done or are doing now and the items you will do in the future. Make a commitment to yourself to act on the items you plan to do in the future. You don't have to do everything on the checklist at once, but refer to it regularly to review the areas in which you can grow.

My Areas for Growth

	I have done or am doing this	I commit myself to doing this in the future
I honestly evaluate the quality and quantity of my work, follow-through, punctuality, and reliability.	_____	_____
I show a positive attitude on the job.	_____	_____
I ask for feedback from my supervisor on a regular basis on specific areas of strengths and weaknesses.	_____	_____
I accept feedback from customers and coworkers on my performance.	_____	_____
I set my own performance goals or ask my supervisor to help me.	_____	_____
When evaluated, I try to identify areas and opportunities for growth.	_____	_____
I let my supervisor know what I have accomplished.	_____	_____
I take advantage of company-offered training.	_____	_____
I get training, when available, on my own time.	_____	_____
I get involved with company-paid classes or tuition reimbursement programs.	_____	_____
I volunteer for new assignments, especially if they involve learning new skills.	_____	_____
I volunteer for more responsibility.	_____	_____

Getting Training and Education

As you've explored careers, you may have decided you need to improve some basic skills. Many schools have classes, tutoring, and learning labs available to help you be more successful in your training program. Find out what is available and where it is located.

Training and educational options include

- **On-the-job training.** This option gives workers a chance to develop skills for a specialized job. On-the-job training is generally offered to new employees who initially do not have the skills to do a job. It may also be offered to experienced employees who are learning new skills needed for job advancement. On-the-job training may involve classroom instruction or hands-on activity or both.

> Schools, colleges and universities, community agencies, or government services may have job-seeking programs in your area. Check your local library or newspaper for schedule information.

- **Apprenticeship programs.** This is a way for unskilled workers to become qualified in a chosen trade. Apprenticeships are usually part of a formal program that combines on-the-job training and classroom instruction. Depending on the career, apprenticeship programs can last from one to six years. Formal testing may be required for an employee to be recognized as qualified.

- **Vocational and technical schools.** These programs provide an excellent way for employees to learn job skills. Classes are generally available beginning at a high-school level. Few courses provide general education requirements; most focus instead on skills related to a particular job. These schools offer certificates of achievement or two-year degrees.

- **U.S. Armed Forces.** The military offers a variety of learning opportunities. People often enter the various armed services to receive job training they can use as civilians. Others take advantage of tuition-aid programs that pay for college or technical training.

- **Informal training.** This kind of training is offered through most community education programs and takes place in a classroom environment. Participants may receive a certificate of completion, but the courses typically do not give formal credit. Even so, they can provide enough information to help employees develop or learn specific skills.

If you find you need more training in job-seeking techniques, look for books in the library or at a nearby bookstore. Videotapes and DVDs also may be available in your library. Check the copyright dates to be sure the material you use is up to date. Job-seeking resources can provide materials such as sample resumes for a variety of jobs, various resume formats for you to consider, resume writing dos and don'ts, sample cover letters, and information about networking and interviewing.

Remember, schools, colleges and universities, community agencies, or government services may have job-seeking programs in your area. Check your local library or newspaper for schedule information.

The following worksheet gives you an idea of what to look for and questions to ask. It lists some practical arrangements you need to make, such as transportation, day care, and the purchase or borrowing of books and equipment. You may not need to do everything on the list. For those activities you want to accomplish, fill in a target date. Check off each task as you complete it. Find out what crucial deadlines and procedures you need to be aware of to avoid delaying your training and education plans.

My Training and Education Checklist

Activity	Target Date	Completed
Obtain a schedule of courses or training programs	_____	_____
Find out how courses are taught (lecture, hands on, or group discussion)	_____	_____
Find out the length of the program	_____	_____
Find out how many people get jobs after completing the program (placement rate)	_____	_____
Find out if help is available to help students find work after completing the program	_____	_____
Meet with an instructor to get more information about the program	_____	_____
Ask about costs and fees	_____	_____
Ask about the application procedure and deadlines	_____	_____
Ask people to serve as references	_____	_____
File the application by the deadline	_____	_____
Inquire about financial aid	_____	_____
Make arrangements for transportation	_____	_____
Make arrangements for uniforms	_____	_____
Make arrangements for equipment	_____	_____
Make arrangements for books	_____	_____
Make arrangements for day care	_____	_____
Find out when classes start and where they will be held	_____	_____

Some important things I need to remember as I continue my training or education:

_____

_____

_____

_____

Ten Keys to Success

Here's a final thought. Memorize the words below. Each begins with one of the letters in the sentence "I do it right." Ten keys to success are

- **Integrity.** This means always being honest. Stand by your principles. Don't change your principles to fit the situation.

- **Determination.** This means making up your mind to be successful. Believe in the inevitability of success. Don't allow anything to stand in your way.

- **Openness.** This means accepting the possibility that ideas can come from anyone or anywhere. Being open to people, ideas, and situations broadens your options and widens your perspective.

- **Initiative.** This means acting independently when necessary. Make a plan and begin working on it. Revise and change it as needed. Don't wait until your plan is perfect—it never will be.

- **Time management.** This means that you work on what is most important rather than on what is most pressing.

- **Resilience.** This means getting back up when setbacks knock you down. Everyone fails sometime. Don't allow challenges to stop you or blur your vision of success. In the face of apparent failure, plan again. Revise and adjust as required. Recommit to your vision. Reaffirm your self-confidence.

- **Imagination.** This means seeing the future in advance. Develop and maintain the perspective of a child. Ask questions such as, "Why not?" and "What if?" Many successes come from seeing an old idea in a new way.

- **Gratitude.** This means actively thanking other people. Say thank-you for every act of generosity or kindness. Pass on to others the same help and prosperity you have received.

- **Humility.** This means recognizing that success is usually the result of the efforts and cooperation of many people. It is seldom the product of just one person's actions.

- **Thinking of others first.** This means using your abilities to benefit people with whom you have contact. Find a way to serve others.

▶ *LET'S REVIEW*

This final checklist will help you evaluate your career-planning and job-seeking skills. Put a check mark next to the items you have learned to do.

Self-Assessment Checklist

_____ I have made a career plan and can identify its components.

_____ I know how to fill out a job application in a way that will impress employers.

_____ I have gathered the information I need for writing my resume, and I know how to use a resume.

_____ I know how to write a cover letter and what information to include.

_____ I have practiced making telephone calls to employers.

_____ I know how to research a company prior to a job interview, and have practiced answering possible interview questions.

_____ I understand the importance of following up on my job seeking activities.

_____ I know factors to consider in evaluating job offers.

_____ I understand how to evaluate my progress.

_____ I can name several actions that are important for me to take to keep my job.

Date: _____

Index